WA

Nigel Cumberland

The Teach Yourself series has been trusted around the world for over 60 years. This series of 'In A Week' business books is designed to help people at all levels and around the world to further their careers. Learn in a week, what the experts learn in a lifetime.

Nigel has spent more than 20 years working all over the world, with the past 10 years spent in the executive coaching and leadership training field. He had previously worked as a finance director with Coats plc, where he managed global multicultural teams, and he has also built up high-performing teams for some of the world's leading recruitment firms: Adecco SA, Hays plc and Harvey Nash plc. In addition, he created his own award-winning recruitment firm in Hong Kong and China, St George's, which was later sold to Hays plc.

Today Nigel runs a talent and leadership training and coaching consultancy called the Silk Road Partnership. He regularly consults, gives workshops, and lectures to organizations on how to optimally develop and grow leaders and talent.

Because of his extensive worldwide experience, Nigel understands the global and cultural issues and challenges of creating, motivating and leading teams – in locations as diverse as Hong Kong, Budapest, Guatemala City, Kuala Lumpur, Shanghai and Dubai.

He was educated at Cambridge University, is a Founding Fellow of the Institute of Coaching Professional Association (ICPA), a Harvard Medical School affiliate and has Certified Practitioner status with the International Association of Coaching (USA). He is also a Fellow of the Institute of Leadership and Management (UK) and a Fellow of the Chartered Institute of Management Accountants (UK).

Nigel currently lives in Dubai and Kuala Lumpur with his wife, Evelyn, son, Zeb, and stepdaughter, Yasmine.

Managing Teams

Nigel Cumberland

www.inaweek.co.uk

Teach Yourself®

Contents

Introduction

'There is no "i" in team but there is in win.'

Michael Jordan

The recent 2012 London Olympics displayed many excellent winning teams showing brilliance in how they worked together. We saw great team coordination, team spirit, focus on collective goals and a unity in how they worked to achieve their goals. Some of the teams had outstanding individuals in their teams who were also great team players. When watching such teams perform, we are awestruck by the beauty and efficiency of these Olympian teams' performances. After reading this book, you will be able to create and lead a team full of such Olympian types with an Olympic team spirit!

Very few people can succeed in their careers without having to manage, supervise and lead other people. Exceptions might include specialists in their fields who are able to grow in their chosen careers without needing to manage anyone. But virtually everyone is part of a team, and at some point in their working lives they must take a leadership role – if only to chair a team meeting or a project in their boss' absence.

Leading a group of people in a team involves many variables, including each team member's personality, expectations, experience and ambitions. Putting a group of people together can produce all kinds of outcomes – sometimes negative (such as conflicts, arguments, poor performance etc) and sometimes positive (great synergy, alignment, great results etc). The role of a team leader or manager is to minimize any potential negative outcomes while maximizing the positive potential of the team.

In seven chapters, this book will walk you through the entire process of successfully leading and managing a team, showing you the key dos and don'ts and spelling out where you need to put special attention and focus. These seven chapters will cover:

How to get started with a team, exploring what a great team looks like and how it performs, and how to create a new team from scratch with individuals who bring their own habits, skills and expectations

The stages of development of a team and how a new manager can gain the respect and understanding of a team

The importance of aligning a team and setting common goals and expectations with clear agreement on a mission, vision and values.

How to create a team culture and processes of excellent communication, with clearly understood expectations, well-run team meetings and discussions, and the minimizing of any conflict and gossip

How to work with remote or virtual team members where face-to-face meetings are difficult to arrange

How to identify and work with problematic and non-performing members of your team and how to balance fairness and discipline

How to ensure that each team member's job role is clear and that the work is efficiently delegated and shared among the team members

How to grow your team through excellent training and development, including coaching, mentoring and on-the-job training

Turning a good team into a team with a culture of excellence

How to create a self-functioning team which can operate in your absence and in which you have groomed a successor to take over from you if needed.

SUNDAY

Getting started with your team

The first step in learning to successfully lead and manage a team is to understand the secrets of being a team leader, whether of an existing team or a team you are creating from scratch. Often you will face a combination of the two, taking over an existing team while also being expected to change its members.

To create a great team, one must first be able to visualize what a high-performing team is like, what goals and objectives such a team aims to achieve, how it works towards achieving these goals and what makes it appear successful.

A second key aspect of creating a new team or joining a team as its leader is understanding that a team grows and develops over time and that its issues, challenges and performance will be strongly influenced by the stage that it has reached in its development.

This chapter will show you how to:

- Understand what teams are and why we need them
- Think through what team excellence looks and feels like
- Create a new team from scratch, exploring the key dos and don'ts
- Apply Tuckman's 'stages of a team' model
- Take over an existing team, gaining its respect and understanding

What are teams and why do we need them?

> '*Talent wins games, but teamwork and intelligence wins championships.*'
> Michael Jordan

> '*Overcoming barriers to performance is how groups become teams.*'
> Katzenbach and Smith

A team can be defined as a group of individuals who are brought together and organized to work together to achieve common collective aims, purposes, objectives or goals. One could argue that if the team has no common objectives or goals, it is simply a group of individuals who just happen to be sharing the same office or job titles.

What makes a team great?

Take a moment to think of a great team, perhaps one you watched during the Olympic Games or a team you have worked in.

What makes your chosen team appear to be a great one?

- Is it because of what they have achieved? Do they achieve far more than other similar teams? Do they always achieve perfect results?
- What skills and knowledge do the team's members possess which might make them stand out?
- Is it because of who is in the team? Does it comprise some high-performing individuals?
- Is it because of how they work together? Do they appear to be aligned? Do they appear to work very positively together?
- Is it because of how they are led and managed? Has the team's leader been in the same role for a long time?
- Is it a team that you wish to be part of? Do you think that you would excel in such a team?

How do you like being managed?

In addition to exploring what makes a team appear like a great and successful one, it is helpful to think about your experiences of being in a team and how those teams were led and managed. Think back and reflect on the bosses you have had in the recent past and then answer the following two questions:

1 In what ways were you and your colleagues managed which inspired and motivated you to want to be in the team, to work harder and generally to feel valued?
2 In what ways were you and your colleagues managed that you did not like and which did not motivate you or inspire you to want to work hard and be in the team?

Answers typically include the following kinds of responses:

Q1: Positive ways of being managed	Q2: Negative ways of being managed
Recognized members of the team for their good performance	Showed too much favouritism to certain members of the team
Openly communicated and talked with all of us	Team meetings were too long and boring

(Continued)

Listened well to our ideas and concerns and gave credit where due	Took credit for all of our effort and work
Recognized the individuality of each of us in the team	Always seemed to delegate all of his/her work to us without ever really explaining what we had to do

Keep a list of your answers to serve as a reminder ensuring that you only repeat the positive habits of your current and past bosses and not their negative ways of managing their teams.

The aim of this book is to ensure that your staff will view you very positively as their boss and, if asked to answer the same two questions, would give a list of positives far longer than any list of negatives!

Understanding the stages of a team

We all change and evolve over time and it is to be hoped as we grow through childhood into adulthood that we will grow not only in age but also positively in terms of our personality, experience and skills.

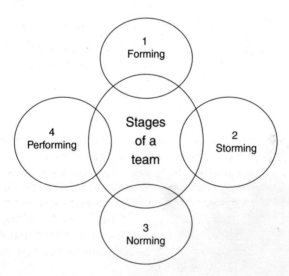

Given that a team is made up of individuals, it should not surprise you to learn that teams also go through different stages of development, from being created through to becoming a mature and, hopefully, high-performing team.

One model of such team development is key to your understanding of teams. It is called the Tuckman model and it is made up of four stages describing a team's development:

Stage 1: Forming

Sometimes called the infant or child stage of a team's development, Stage 1 occurs when a team is newly created or 'born'. During this stage the new team's members are learning their way together and it is sometimes called a period of testing and dependence where the necessary processes, norms and common understandings are not yet in place.

A leader of a forming team may typically observe and experience the following happening among the team members:

- not knowing who to ask for help or what to do
- cautiousness as people test what is acceptable and needed
- beginning to develop trust in each other
- complaints that things are not what they are used to
- anxiety
- getting to know the common goals and expectations.

Have you experienced working and/or leading a team that is moving through the forming stage? What do you recall about this period?

Stage 2: Storming

Some refer to this stage as the rebellious teenage years of a team's growth and development. This is the most difficult stage for a team and the most challenging for the team's leader. Sadly, many teams get stuck at or revert to this stage. The stage is often identifiable through conflicts and arguments as team members try to assert what they think should be done or said. One could view it as the time when the members think they know what needs to be done and each grows in confidence as their egos clash.

Team members of a storming team may typically:

● express of all kinds of differences
● question the way the team is being led and managed
● attempt to assert their individuality and independence
● exhibit a team performance that declines and slows down
● experience conflict, arguments and fallings out
● form rival groups and engage in office politics
● wish to leave the group, or even resign.

When were you last in a team or leading a team that was passing through such a difficult and turbulent phase of development? How did you respond and cope?

Stage 3: Norming

This is sometimes called the early adulthood stage of the team's development and is typically evidenced by the team becoming more cohesive after having worked through some of the storming-period challenges. There is an emerging understanding and acceptance of the team's goals and working styles, and each person's role and personality.
   The following might be visible within such a team:

● consensus-building and decision-making
● confiding and sharing with each other

- pulling together to achieve the team's goals
- a performance that begins to be good and consistent
- the boundaries of the team having been established.

Has a team that you have been part of ever reached such a stage of maturity and performance? Did you see any evidence of the earlier stages still evident in the team?

Stage 4: Performing

This is the optimal stage and could be called a mature adult stage of development. Not all teams will reach this level, and those that do often relapse into the other stages over time.
   A high-performing team is identified by:

- the unique identity it has established
- interdependence between team members
- how well everything seems to flow
- people seeking new challenges as they sense that everything is straightforward and becoming easy to do
- the team being given more to do, so workloads increase
- a lot of work being accomplished and goals achieved
- members caring about and supporting each other.

Have you ever led or worked in a team that has reached this optimal stage of its development? What do you recall about this time?

It is possible to take an online assessment to work out which stage your team has reached; results usually show a team being at all four stages, although one particular stage is normally dominant.

Based on the description of the four stages of development, at what stage (or stages) is your existing team?

New and existing teams

Are you taking over an existing team or are you being asked to create a completely new team?

- If you have been asked to create a completely new team, your team will be in the 'forming' stage and you might not face the complexity of being simultaneously at different stages.
- If you have been asked to take over an existing team, especially if the team has previously been underperforming, it is likely that the team will be mainly in the 'storming' stage.

In the latter case, what do you think will happen to such a team when you join it as its boss? Typically the team will partially go into a 'forming' stage as you bring new and unknown expectations, working style and goals to the team.

When taking over an existing group of people you need to explore at what stages they are working. Combined with this, as you and any other new team members join the team, there will be a partial return to the 'forming' stage as the whole group is working together for the first time. As a result, such a team is never static and you will be kept very busy as the manager.

A successful leader of any team must continually ensure that the entire team quickly and effectively moves from the 'forming' stage into the 'norming' and 'performing' stages, without getting stuck in the 'storming' stage. Much of this book's advice is focused on ensuring that your team does not become stuck at the 'storming' stage.

Creating a brand new team

1 Hire the ideal talent
You can create the ideal new and optimal working culture (habits, norms etc) through hiring the ideal kinds of individuals.

Do not rush this important process and plan well what kind of team you wish to create. What mix of personalities and skills does your new team need in order to ensure that it succeeds?

2 **Allow time for your team to understand your expectations**
Give the new team members time to get to know your own expectations regarding goals, aims and objectives. Give them more time if they are joining your team from other organizations rather than moving internally within your company. (Monday's chapter explains how to set goals and objectives for your team.)

3 **Be careful with experienced new team members**
Many of your new team will have left established teams to join yours. Such individuals may quickly start to act as if they know what to do (a kind of 'been there, done that' mentality) and as a result your team could very quickly enter the 'storming' phase. Be ready for this and be firm when you observe unacceptable behaviour.

Taking over an existing team in your organization

1 **Be clear about what is unacceptable**
You will be taking over a team with many good and bad habits and working styles which will have been created by the team under their previous manager(s). Your task is to observe quickly and listen well to understand what is happening, and then to map out which habits you wish to either:
- strengthen and support, e.g. good team spirit and communication
- lessen and reduce, e.g. writing long email reports
- stop altogether, e.g. wasting time in meetings
- have the team start doing, e.g. follow a new reporting style.

2 **Be ready for resistance**
The existing team may not readily accept you as their new boss, making comments such as: 'But this is not the way we used to do things ... we used to operate very well.' Remember that people find any kind of change or disruption

hard to accept so a new boss can create anxiety and concern and they will fight to hold on to the past (i.e. ways in which they were previously managed). Be patient, explain clearly your rationale for any changes but be firm when necessary.

3 **Be ready to communicate clearly**
The team will be used to working in a certain way and now they have a new boss. As a result you will need to be especially mindful of the need to communicate clearly about what you are observing and expecting of the team. (Such communication challenges are covered in Tuesday's chapter.)

Taking over a team in a new organization

When you move to a new company as a team manager, all of the above advice applies, and there are a few additional points to remember as well.

1 **Adapt to the new culture and working norms**
You will need to align your own working and leadership styles with the norms and expectations of your new organization and of your own new boss. Do not go charging into your role using your previous style. You may need to alter, tone down or emphasize certain aspects of your management style. Observe what is different in your new company compared with your previous experiences.

2 **Work to gain your team's respect and acceptance**
You must remember that you are the new person in the team and you may face resistance to being accepted. Be ready to be patient, listen exceptionally well and ask as many questions as possible to ensure that you are understood and also that you truly understand the norms and expectations of your new organization and its culture.

Summary

You now understand what a team is and what makes a team great.

We have explored how you like to be managed and led, which can help guide you in how you choose to manage others, e.g. not copying a past boss's bad habits!

You can now use the Tuckman model, which helps you to understand which of the four stages of development your team has reached – forming, storming, norming or performing.

You now understand the key challenges of starting to manage a completely new team and taking over an established team.

We have also discussed the challenges of taking over a team in a new organization that you might have joined.

Now that you understand how to start managing a team, you are ready to learn how to become a successful manager and in the Monday chapter we will explore how you can ensure that your team is aligned with a clear mission, vision, value and goals.

SUNDAY

MONDAY

TUESDAY

WEDNESDAY

THURSDAY

FRIDAY

SATURDAY

Fact-check (answers at the back)

1. Which of the following is *not* a stage of the Tuckman model?
a) Norming ❏
b) Feeling ❏
c) Storming ❏
d) Forming ❏

2. Which of the following is *not* a characteristic of a group that is a team?
a) A team has common goals ❏
b) A team is aligned ❏
c) A team works together ❏
d) A team does not communicate together ❏

3. How would you best describe a team at the forming stage of development?
a) It has been established a long time ❏
b) It has very few members ❏
c) It is a newly created team ❏
d) It is a virtual team ❏

4. What is a key difference between teams at the storming and at the norming stages?
a) A storming team is not performing well but a norming team is ❏
b) A norming team is more recently formed than a storming team ❏
c) A storming team is more productive than a norming team ❏
d) Both are very similar ❏

5. What are the challenges of starting to lead a team in a company that you have just joined?
a) You have less time to perform your work well ❏
b) You don't know the company's and the team's culture and norms ❏
c) You have no specific challenges ❏
d) Members of your team do not know each other ❏

6. Which stage of a team's growth and development should you be aiming for?
a) Storming ❏
b) Performing ❏
c) Forming ❏
d) Norming ❏

7. Which of the following is *not* a characteristic of a performing team?
a) Everything seems to flow well ❏
b) A unique identity has been established ❏
c) Arguments between members ❏
d) Interdependence has been created ❏

8. Which of the following is very unusual in a team in the storming phase?
a) People trying to assert their individuality and independence ❑
b) Performance of the team declining and slowing down ❑
c) Conflicts, arguments and falling out ❑
d) The team is in alignment and agrees on most things ❑

9. Which of the following would you expect of a newly created team in the forming stage?
a) Complaints that things are not what they are used to ❑
b) Anxiety ❑
c) Getting to know the common goals and expectations ❑
d) All of the above ❑

10. When taking over a new team, why is it important to listen and ask questions?
a) Because you need to truly understand what is happening and what members of the team are thinking and doing ❑
b) Because people only like a boss who listens and does not tell them what to do ❑
c) Because you have no time to do anything else ❑
d) Because you do not know what else you could do ❑

MONDAY

Alignment and goal-setting for your team

The Sunday chapter introduced you to the various stages that your team may have reached. It is now time to explore how you will align your team around a particular direction, purpose and goals. It is no good creating a team and then leaving it to do its own thing without a clear idea of where it is heading or what its goals are.

This chapter will explain how to:

- Create mission and vision statements that show the purpose and direction of the team
- Set clear and achievable goals, both for the team as a whole and for individual team members
- Understand why and how your goals or objectives should be **SMART**, **CLEAR** and **PURE**
- Use the goal-setting process to give a new team some quick wins that will help the team-bonding process
- Create a team charter to outline your team's purpose and clarify how the team will work together
- Emphasize the importance of alignment within a team to ensure that individuals' goals and aims are in line with yours and those of the organization
- Ensure that your team's understandings and expectations are in alignment with yours.

Setting a direction for your team

'The trouble with not having a goal is that you can spend your life running up and down the field and never score.'

Bill Copeland

'If everyone is moving forward together, then success takes care of itself.'

Henry Ford

Imagine being asked to lead a team of people in a company that you have just joined. Now imagine if nobody in the company had answers if you asked the following questions.

- What are the goals for my team this year?
- How will we know if my team has done a good job this month?
- What are the aims and the objectives of my team?
- What is the mission and vision of my team and of the company?
- What values are expected or need to be exhibited by my team?
- What kind of culture does my team have?

Often, managers are not clear about their team's direction, just doing the work and tasks that seem urgent and important and responding to other colleagues' and stakeholders' requests and needs. Do you know what I mean? Being very busy, but not really being productive or having a clear direction to your work?

A successful team manager must set the direction of the team, specifically by:

- creating the mission and vision of the team
- developing a set of team values
- developing an optimal team culture
- setting the goals and objectives that the team needs to achieve
- formulating a team charter.

Creating a mission and vision for your team

What is a team's mission? This is a statement of purpose about why the team exists. Here are some examples of possible team mission statements.

- We are a team of SAP implementation experts working to roll out SAP in a timely and cost-effective manner in the company (a SAP implementation team in a company's IT department)
- We exist to ensure that the company's internal audit processes and controls are optimized and robust (an internal audit team)
- We are a top-performing marketing department able to successfully help roll out and support all of our company's existing and new product lines (a multinational's marketing function).

What is a team's vision? It is often seen as a description of what the team wishes to become in the future. Here are some examples of team vision statements.

- To become the leading accounting and finance support team in the entire company (a finance and accounting team)
- To be the highest-performing sales team in the industry (a regional or product sales team)
- To be the team that everyone turns to for advice and help on taxation (a taxation team in a company's finance function).

Often the mission and vision are merged into one statement or paragraph.

Do you have such statements for your team? Why not work with your new team to develop mission and vision statements.

Team mission and vision statements should be aligned with the organization's own purpose and direction to avoid your team pulling in the wrong direction.

Developing a set of team values

A team's values show what the team stands for and believes in. They are the attitudes, beliefs and behaviours that matter to the individuals in the team. We all have values but the question is: are we conscious of what our values are and are they optimized to help the team to succeed?

Studies show that organizations and teams that have thoughtful, positive and aligned sets of values are able to operate and perform more successfully. Not surprisingly, a team that is poorly managed or led often develops negative or unproductive values which can impact badly upon the team's performance. Examples of such values might include:

- that it is OK to be late
- that there is no need to take responsibility
- not listening to others

- keeping others under pressure
- not sharing information unless asked.

What are your own values? And what values do you wish your team to have and to live and work by? Does your organization or your boss have a list of core values that they expect you and your team to live by?

Here are some typical examples of values that various organizations and teams aspire to work and live by:

- honesty and integrity
- open communication
- taking full responsibility
- thinking out of the box and being creative
- being persistent and never giving up
- always helping and giving time to others
- working with passion and enthusiasm
- always being willing to listen and be open-minded
- being technically up-to-date and knowledgeable.

Do aim to develop a list of values for your team, and be ready to work with team members in turning the values into habits which form part of how you work together each day.

Developing an optimal team culture

Culture and values are interconnected; the culture could best be defined as the collective behaviour and patterns of the individuals in the team. It is normally made up of their values as well as their habits, behaviours, beliefs, working norms, expectations and communication styles. Put simply, it is how the team chooses to act, think and operate.

I strongly advise you to ensure that the culture you create, support and grow within the team that you lead is consciously developed and is optimized to ensure your team's success.

Setting team goals and objectives

Having set the direction for your team, it is now key to set the team's goals and objectives. Goals and objectives are much the same things, and often goals are expressed as Key Performance Indicators (KPIs).

Sometimes the goals for your team are set by your boss or others in your organization. In this case, you would normally still have the responsibility of breaking down the team-wide goals to create individual goals for each member of your team. Have you done this before, and how easy was this for you?

When setting goals for individuals in a team it is important to demonstrate that you did so thoughtfully and objectively. I like to use the following framework, which comprises 14 requirements of optimal goals: **SMART, CLEAR** and **PURE**. This model is attributed to the British leadership coach John Whitmore.

Do use this framework as a checklist when you next need to create or to review the goals of your team:

Optimal goals are **SMART**:

Which means the goals are:	How do you ensure this?
Specific	Goals should be clearly stated and relate to specific aspects of the team's work
Measurable	Goals should be as objective and quantifiable as possible
Attainable	Bear in mind the saying: 'If a goal is unattainable there is no hope, and if it is not challenging it is not motivating.'
Realistic	Goals should be relevant and realistically related to the team's work
Timely	Goals should be achievable in the time frame set for achieving them

Optimal goals are **PURE**:

Which means the goals are:	How do you ensure this?
Positive	Goals should be expressed, as far as possible, as positive rather than negative achievements
Understood	Goals should be understandable by your team, otherwise they will never be able to accept them
Relevant	Goals should be relevant to what your team are employed to do
Ethical	Goals should not force your team to question their integrity, e.g. having to consider cheating to achieve the goal

Optimal goals are **CLEAR**:

Which means the goals are:	How do you ensure this?
Challenging	Goals should be challenging to motivate your team
Legal	Goals must be legally acceptable, just as they should be ethical
Environmentally friendly	Goals should not involving wasting resources or adversely affecting the environment
Agreed	Goals should be agreed and accepted by those asked to achieve them
Recorded	Goals should be written down and shared, with people signing off on them as needed

Do not let the goal-setting model complicate your thinking. Remember the popular acronym K.I.S.S. ('Keep it simple, Stupid!'). If in doubt, keep the goal simple – it is better to achieve something rather than nothing at all.

Goal-setting with a new team

When setting goals with a new team for the first time, you need to be especially careful and mindful of the fact that you may not yet have built up high levels of mutual trust, understanding and rapport. Bear in mind the following.

1 **Have some quick-win goals**
Try to set some collective team goals which can be achieved relatively easily and quickly. These wins will enable your team to celebrate some success together quickly and show team members that under your leadership the team is on the right track. This should help you bond with the team and gain their respect and confidence.
2 **Spend extra time explaining your proposed goals**
Be ready to spend extra time explaining the logic and rationale for the goals or objectives that you are setting or accepting (from your boss or others in your organization). Remember that some people will not openly say that they do not agree with or buy into your goals.

Formulating a team charter

A team charter summarizes the scope of the team's work, what the team needs to achieve and how it will do so, including establishing the boundaries of the team's work.

There are no fixed rules for a team charter's content, but I would suggest as a starting point a structure such as the following.

Ideal headings within your team charter	Details
What is our team purpose?	This is your team's mission and vision
What are our desired end results and goals?	These are your team's goals and objectives
How will the team work together?	List how the team members will interact, work and communicate together
Who are our key stakeholders?	Listing out all the key stakeholders and how the team needs to work with each of them

Do consider spending a few hours with your new team creating your first team charter.

Aligning your team

Visualize a rowing team – it might be one of the teams in the annual Oxford and Cambridge University Boat Race. Perhaps there are eight or even 12 rowers, with a cox steering the boat. How can the team ensure that it wins the race?

Scenario 1 – By each person rowing at his own pace and as fast as he can, ignoring the others in the boat, including the cox?

Scenario 2 – By each person rowing at the same rate and in perfect formation, with the oars entering and leaving the water at the same time, and being guided by the instructions of the cox about when to speed up or slow down?

I do hope that you chose the second scenario as the correct answer!

A team's alignment can be defined as having a group of individuals who all understand and agree to:

- the team's direction and purpose, e.g. mission statement, vision statement, values and/or strategic direction, team charter (already covered in this chapter)
- the team's goals and objectives for the current and/or next financial year or period – I hope after reading this chapter you have a clear idea of how and why goal-setting is so important
- individual job responsibilities, duties and goals (see the Tuesday chapter)

- the team's working style and norms, e.g. communication styles, meeting protocols etc (other chapters will explore these in more detail).

Why is team alignment so important?

A team that is not aligned could also be called a dysfunctional team. Such teams exhibit a range of unproductive working styles and behaviours, including:

- wasting time and other resources – the team may be working unproductively, e.g. work may being replicated or may be taking too long to complete
- arguments and misunderstandings – different members of the team may have widely divergent beliefs and expectations
- sabotage and deception – team members might play games, e.g. withholding information from one another.

If you take over an existing team and you spot any of the above behaviours and outcomes, you will need to analyse why the team is not aligned and then decide how to rectify the causes of any misalignment.

A final question on this alignment topic is related to you as the team's leader: are you really and genuinely aligned with your boss and your organization?

- Do you agree with and buy into your boss's and organization's directions, values, culture, goals etc?
- Are you willing and able to change your own beliefs, values, goals etc so that they are in alignment with what your boss and your organization ask and expect of you?
- Are you then able to create and develop the optimal direction and goals for yourself and for your team, which are in alignment with your boss's and your organization's needs and expectations?

You might welcome the help of an executive coach or mentor, or relevant training courses, to help you to understand how to align your own thinking and beliefs so that your team can literally follow your lead, rather than being expected to 'do as I say and not as I do (or believe)'.

- You cannot expect people to always complete their work on time if you leave tasks unfinished.
- You cannot ask your team to always arrive early for client presentations if you are often late.

If you wish to change your team's behaviours, culture etc, try to follow the words of Mahatma Gandhi:

'Be the change that you want to see in the world.'

SUNDAY MONDAY TUESDAY WEDNESDAY THURSDAY FRIDAY SATURDAY

Summary

As the working world becomes ever more complex, with a 24/7 culture of Blackberries and emails, a team could easily find itself overwhelmed, overworked and not knowing what to do next. As their manager it is your role to give your team clarity of purpose and direction, and to keep them all aligned with clear goals and expectations of the values and culture that they must aspire to work by.

You are now in a good position to create a direction and purpose for your team in the form of mission and vision statements; develop the required values and culture within your team; and decide if you wish to work with your team to create a team charter.

You can appreciate the importance of being aligned as a team and all rowing your 'boat' as one team.

You understand the importance of you, as the team's leader, 'walking the talk' and doing what you expect of others in your team.

The next stage is to assign responsibilities and delegate work within your team and to ensure that the work is optimally allocated so that the team is as productive as possible. This is the subject of Tuesday's chapter.

Fact-check (answers at the back)

1. What is a mission statement?
   a) A statement of past performance ❏
   b) A statement of purpose ❏
   c) A statement of working hours ❏
   d) All of above ❏

2. What is a vision statement?
   a) A statement of what you wish to become in the future ❏
   b) A statement of the future planned budget forecast ❏
   c) A statement summarizing feedback from the team members ❏
   d) None of the above ❏

3. Why is alignment important?
   a) It makes a team more productive ❏
   b) It reduces duplication and wasted effort ❏
   c) It avoids arguments ❏
   d) All of above ❏

4. A team charter might include:
   a) Goals ❏
   b) Purpose ❏
   c) Working norms ❏
   d) All of the above ❏

5. What is the culture of a team?
   a) An organigram ❏
   b) Behaviours and habits ❏
   c) Salary and remuneration scale ❏
   d) Working hours and overtime rules ❏

6. Which of the following are possible values of a team?
   a) Honesty ❏
   b) Good listening ❏
   c) Persistence ❏
   d) All of the above ❏

7. Which of the following is *not* a SMART goal requirement?
   a) Creative ❏
   b) Timely ❏
   c) Measurable ❏
   d) Realistic ❏

8. Which of the following is *not* a CLEAR goal requirement?
   a) Agreed ❏
   b) Recorded ❏
   c) Detailed ❏
   d) Legal ❏

9. Which of the following is a PURE goal requirement?
   a) Short ❏
   b) Written in English ❏
   c) Complex ❏
   d) Relevant ❏

10. What does K.I.S.S. mean? ❏
    a) Be loving and kind ❏
    b) Keep it simple, Stupid ❏
    c) Know Information Simply Stated ❏
    d) None of the above

TUESDAY

Delegating and managing the work within your team

The Sunday and Monday chapters have discussed how to take over a new team, the different stages of team development and how to set your team's direction and goals. This has created a framework that allows you to get the team as a whole into an optimal shape or alignment. We will now explore how to ensure that each individual member of your team is able to perform his or her role optimally.

This chapter will show you how to:

- Place the right people in roles that suit their interests, personality, skills and experience
- Use a model to understand the typical kinds of work-role preferences that different people might have
- Delegate and allocate work to your team to ensure that the work is completed and that the work is shared fairly
- Ensure that individuals' goals and key performance indicators are in alignment with the team's and organization's goals
- Engage with, empower and motivate your team so that they will succeed in ways above and beyond what is expected of them.

Managing the individuals in your team

> *'An empowered organization is one in which individuals have the knowledge, skill, desire, and opportunity to personally succeed in a way that leads to collective organizational success.'*
>
> Stephen Covey

A participant in a management training course that I was leading recently said that he would rather be in charge of 100 machines than be in charge of just one person. That may sound extreme but many managers, even those with many years of experience in leading others, can feel overwhelmed by the prospect of having to manage and deal with the individuals in their team.

A key role of anyone leading a team is to ensure that each member of the team:

- is placed in the optimal job role
- understands what to do
- knows why it needs doing
- understands how to do it
- is able to do it
- actually wants to do it.

I have developed the following six-step framework to help you ensure that each person in a team is given every possible chance of being a successful performer and contributor who will hopefully stay with the team.

The six-step team talent management framework

In many ways being a great manager is learning to ask the right questions, rather than knowing the answers. The 'six steps' are in the form of six questions which you are strongly encouraged to ask yourself whenever you face challenges in managing members of your team.

Who	• Step 1. WHO do you place in each role within your team?
Why	• Step 2. Does each person in your team know WHY the team is taking a particular direction?
What	• Step 3. Does each person in your team know WHAT they must do?
How	• Step 4. Does each member of your team know HOW to do their work?
Can	• Step 5. CAN each team member successfully complete their work and achieve their goals?
Want	• Step 6. Does each of your team WANT to work in their job and in your team?

The remainder of this chapter will walk you through this important model.

Step 1. WHO do you place in each role within your team?

Before determining what work, task and goals each team member needs to complete, you must first ensure that you have the ideal people in each job role.

I once hired an accountant to work in my team and for a couple of years she did a great job. She was a highly qualified accountant with a stellar track record. Then one day she made a serious mistake in a spreadsheet that she had created. When she came to apologize we began talking about how tedious and sometimes boring being an accountant can be. She then revealed that she did not enjoy her job any more and that was probably why she was making mistakes. She spoke of preferring job roles that would be more people-focused and customer-facing. Luckily I was able to offer her a customer service role which she enjoyed and performed well. She is not unique; so many people work in jobs that they either do not enjoy and/or are not very good at. Can you imagine how unproductive your team would be if it were filled with such people?

As a manager you must ensure that each role is filled by the ideal individual – someone who is able, motivated and willing to perform well in that role. You must decide the criteria team members must meet in order to perform well in your team as well as in specific roles.

- What are the required hard skills, such as work experience, technical and academic experience and skills? How suitable is the person?
- What kind of soft skills or attitudes, behaviour and personality are needed? How suitable is the person?
- Do you need to analyse further the required tasks and responsibilities of the role? Do you have job descriptions that are sufficiently detailed?
- Do you wish to adjust the job role to fit a potentially strong member of your team?

When hiring people or considering changes to an existing member's role, you should draw up a list of key job requirements. You can then carry out a gap analysis to understand where the individual may fall short and where they are strong. Examples might include:

- lacking certain technical experience or certification
- not having enough product or industry exposure
- not possessing the ideal soft skills, e.g. not sufficiently persistent or details-oriented.

Then ask yourself:

1 Do their strengths and potential outweigh their weaknesses?
2 Can I help to develop their areas of weakness while strengthening their strengths?

Suitability is a key success or failure factor

I have come to realize that a major weakness of most under-performing teams is having people in roles for which they are not suited. The reason is that each of us has a natural preference for the kind of work we enjoy doing, e.g. some like to plan, others like to move around, while others prefer to delegate work.

To be a successful manager, you need to ensure that each person is ideally suited to the work you wish them to do. How can you do this? You need to understand the individual's work preferences, and this can achieved through observation, interview or using an assessment tool. There are many assessment tools, including the Belbin Team Roles Inventory, Harrison Assessment, Gallup's Strengths Finder and SHL's OPQ; we shall look at the Belbin model.

Exploring preferences using the Belbin model

This model, created by the psychologist Meredith Belbin, is used to discover what kind of work tasks we like to do. It demonstrates that we all prefer one or more of the following nine kinds of roles.

Role title	Role description
Shaper	Prefers roles in which they can seek improvements and challenge others to improve
Implementer	Prefers work in which ideas and plans have to be put into action

(Continued)

Completer finisher	Prefers work which involves finishing things, often thoroughly and in a timely way
Coordinator	Prefers to act as someone coordinating others' actions and often likes to take charge of meetings
Team worker	Prefers roles that work closely with others and would not like a solitary role
Resource investigator	Prefers work that involves research and gathering information
Planter	Prefers work that involves having to develop new approaches and ideas
Monitor evaluator	Prefers work involving analysis and analysing information and options
Specialist	Prefers work that enables them to be an expert in a certain area or field

Based on the nine Belbin roles, what are your preferred work role preferences? What are those of your team members?

As you use such a model, you will make all sorts of discoveries. A typical example might be discovering that the person in your team who never completes their work on time might have the 'Completer finisher' role very low in their preferences profile. When faced with such an example of what I call a misfit, you can:

● encourage the person to develop and change
● change the role for the person
● change the person, i.e. replace him or her.

You can find a free version of the Belbin model on the internet. Do explore using such an assessment to understand your team members and yourself better.

Step 2. Does each person in your team know WHY the team is taking a particular direction?

Monday's chapter showed you how to ensure that your team has a clear direction through having a stated mission, vision, team charter, and team goals and objectives. But do your team members understand how each of their roles and work can contribute towards helping the team to achieve these things?

Your team may claim to know and agree but there is no harm in checking. In your next team meeting, ask your team questions such as:

- How would you describe our team's objectives, purpose and goals? Are they clear enough?
- Can you recite our team mission and vision statements? Do you like them? How can we word them differently?
- How does your role contribute to the team's and to the organization's success?

Step 3. Does each person in your team know WHAT they must do?

Individual and shared goals

Monday's chapter showed you how to create goals for your team. You might also create Key Performance Indicators (KPIs) for each team member – these are goals written in the form of measures against which performance can be measured.

As a manager you need to decide:

- which of the team goals are shared by the entire team
- which team goals can be broken down into individual goals
- how to ensure that individual goals are aligned with the overall team goals that your boss or organization may have given you.

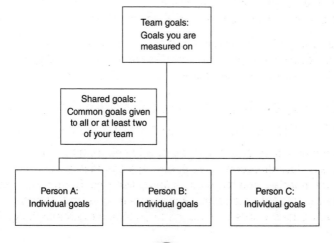

The kinds of goals that you set will vary by the function, industry and organization that your team is part of.

- How difficult should the goals be to achieve? Much is written about having challenging goals and it is your task to decide how easy or demanding the goals should be. My advice would be to make them difficult but also achievable – so-called stretch goals
- How will you motivate your team to achieve their goals? This would be through a combination of monetary and non-monetary incentives, which we explore later in this chapter.

Job description, responsibilities and duties

The goals given to an individual should correlate with their job description. Does each of your team have a clear job description which enables them to understand what is expected of them in terms of performance?

A great job description should include at least two things.

1 A detailed description of the responsibilities and tasks
2 A description of the needed competencies, i.e. knowledge, skills, behaviours and attitudes.

Be ready to update and adjust the job descriptions of your team members when you are reviewing their performance and setting their goals and objectives for the following budget year or period. In the Wednesday chapter we will discuss how to evaluate performance and give feedback to each of your team.

Step 4. Does each member of your team know HOW to do their work?

Do they have the right knowledge, skills, attitudes, training and development? There are three aspects to this question.

1 You should know what strengths your team members possess and aim to make full use of them to help your team achieve its goals. This strengths-based leadership approach can be a positive and motivating approach to working with your team.
2 Do your team members have areas of weakness and/or areas that need development to help them perform better

in their roles? You will need to share, diplomatically, your opinions with your team members and help them to plan how they will bridge the gaps.

3 Your team has four options with respect to how they use any of their competencies (their hard and soft skills, knowledge and behaviours etc). These are shown below.

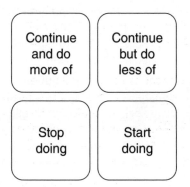

You can be successful as a manager by learning how to evaluate and then communicate to each of your team what they need to do to perform to their maximum potential:

● continue and do more of, e.g. to continue being persistent and detail-oriented
● continue but do less of, e.g. to continue replying to all emails in a timely fashion but to write shorter emails
● stop doing, e.g. to stop interrupting colleagues during their presentations
● start doing, e.g. to start learning about project management and how to lead projects.

Step 5. CAN each team member successfully complete their work and achieve their goals?

Your team might be qualified and very eager to complete their work and to achieve their goals. However:

● do they have the necessary tools, resources, systems, processes and people network?

- even if they have everything they need, are they empowered and allowed to do all that they must to achieve their goals?

I recently coached an individual who complained about not being able to do his job well. He said that, although he had been working in his company for over three months, he had not yet been given a computer or his own work station.

If your team members had no computer or work station, could they succeed in their roles? Does your team have everything it needs to succeed? What might you be overlooking? Such issues will be specific to your team, but here are some examples:

- Do team members understand how to operate your company's enterprise resource planning and other software systems?
- Do team members have a copy of any employee handbook?
- Do team members know who to contact to seek help and assistance within your team or in other departments?

Step 6. Does each of your team WANT to work in their job and in your team?

Are your team members sufficiently engaged and motivated to stay in their roles and to perform well? This is a very important question.

Do you understand what motivates your team (and you)? Much has been studied and written with regard to motivation. The two best-known theories of motivation are:

- Maslow's hierarchy of needs – this states that once the basic human needs (such as food and shelter) are satisfied, a person then seeks things like meaning and to be valued.
- Herzberg's two-factor model – this explains that some things offered to employees, so-called Hygiene Factors such as a person's salary and working conditions, are not positively motivating and are necessary simply to prevent dissatisfaction. According to Herzberg, the things that truly motivate individuals, Motivators, are such things as being valued and being given responsibility.

AT BLOGGS AND SON, THEY GET APPLES AND A PAT ON THE BACK

I think that there is truth in both of these well-known models, but what motivates one person may not motivate another. Everyone is unique, and it is your key task as their manager to explore, learn and act upon what will (or might) motivate each of your team members. What are you offering your team to motivate them to perform well? Here is a list of the kinds of things that might motivate a typical employee. It is not an exhaustive list, but it serves to show you that virtually anything can serve to motivate or demotivate someone in your team:

- monetary rewards
- base salary
- bonuses
- other benefits – statutory and optional
- working hours and overtime
- holidays
- equipment – PC, car, phone
- office space
- office facilities – kitchen, smoking room
- social events and outings
- delegation
- mentorship
- induction programme
- connecting with leaders
- travel
- expenses' reimbursement policy
- overseas postings
- early responsibility
- annual remuneration review
- quality of food in the canteen
- management and supervisory opportunities
- job description and KPIs
- culture
- environment
- responsibility

- challenge
- communication
- growth of business and opportunities
- learning, development and training
- freedom and openness to ideas
- feedback and listening culture
- performance reviews
- promotions
- career path
- equitable workplace
- fair recognition and reward of performance
- diversity and lack of discrimination
- termination process and outplacement

Seven basic needs

When I coach individuals and teams, I am often astonished to discover what is causing individuals to be demotivated (sometimes called disengaged). I have come to believe that all human beings have seven basic needs which have to be met to truly fulfil and motivate them.

Basic needs	Description
To have certainty	People like to know what is happening and what they have to do. We dislike change and the unexpected.
To have variety	People rarely like to do the same monotonous work each day and will become bored.
To be valued	People like to be acknowledged and thanked for their work and contribution.
To connect with others	People rarely like to work completely alone without being able to communicate with others.
To be able to contribute	People want to feel that their efforts and work are worthwhile and for a greater good.
To be able to grow	People like to grow in their careers and roles and to learn more.
To leave a legacy	People like to do things that will make a difference and leave a lasting impression.

I think that you can quickly become a successful manager if you bear in mind these seven needs and try to ensure that what you offer and promise your team members fulfils these.

Do note, though, that not every person will exhibit all seven needs at any one time.

If you are not sure what might motivate your team to perform well, a good starting point is to think about what motivates you. I would also encourage you to ask your team what they seek in life and why they work in your organization and within your team. The answers might surprise you!

Over time, as you become a more experienced manager, you will get a better sense for what can successfully motivate people in your team.

Summary

This chapter has shown you a simple six-part framework to help each of your staff to succeed.

You understand the need to ensure that you give appropriate work to each of your team.

You can make sure that your team understands the direction the team and the organization is taking.

You can work with each member of your team to give them a clear understanding of what they need to do in their work and clear goals and objectives.

You can explore whether each team member has the necessary skills, knowledge and behaviours to undertake their work and to achieve their goals.

You understand the range of tools, resources, systems, processes and people network that your team requires for it to succeed.

You appreciate how to motivate members of your team, realizing the wide array of factors that can motivate and engage each member of your team.

SUNDAY
MONDAY
TUESDAY
WEDNESDAY
THURSDAY
FRIDAY
SATURDAY

Fact-check (answers at the back)

1. What does the 'Who' part of the six-part team talent management framework refer to?
   a) Does your team have the tools they need ❑
   b) Is your team motivated ❑
   c) Is your team communicating well ❑
   d) Matching the ideal people with roles ❑

2. What is Maslow's hierarchy of needs?
   a) A job description framework ❑
   b) A training programme ❑
   c) A model of what motivates people ❑
   d) An organigram structure ❑

3. Which of the following is *not* one of the nine Belbin team roles?
   a) Team worker ❑
   b) Shaper ❑
   c) Implementer ❑
   d) Driver ❑

4. What are shared goals?
   a) Goals for one individual ❑
   b) Goals for more than one team member ❑
   c) Goals for another team ❑
   d) None of the above ❑

5. Which of the following is *not* one of the seven basic needs?
   a) To have certainty ❑
   b) To have time ❑
   c) To be able to grow ❑
   d) To leave a legacy ❑

6. Herzberg's two-factor model states that what two groups of things motivate people?
   a) Motivators and hygiene factors ❑
   b) Hygiene factors and money ❑
   c) Safety factors and time ❑
   d) None of the above ❑

7. A good job description should include:
   a) Job duties ❑
   b) Job responsibilities ❑
   c) Qualification needs ❑
   d) All of the above ❑

8. Which of the following describes the Planter role in Belbin's model?
   a) Prefers work involving analysis and analysing information and options ❑
   b) Prefers work that involves having to develop new approaches and ideas ❑
   c) Prefers work in which ideas and plans have to be put into action ❑
   d) Prefers roles that work closely with others and would not like a solitary role ❑

9. Which of the following describes the need to connect with others?

a) People rarely like to work completely alone without being able to communicate with others ❑

b) People want to feel that their efforts and work are worthwhile and for a greater good ❑

c) People like to grow in their careers and roles and to learn more ❑

d) People like to do things that will make a difference ❑

10. Which of the following describes the need to have variety?

a) People like to know what is happening and what they have to do. We dislike change and the unexpected ❑

b) People rarely like to do the same monotonous work each day and will become bored ❑

c) People like to be acknowledged and thanked for their work and contribution ❑

d) People rarely like to work completely alone without being able to communicate with others ❑

WEDNESDAY

Optimal communication within your team

Your job as a manager is to lead a team with passion and belief, and to inspire them to great performances. Systems and procedures alone are not enough to achieve this and what you need to develop and nurture will be all forms of excellent communication both with and within your team.

All successful managers understand that, no matter the size of their team or business, only through constant and varied types of communication with their staff can they maintain the performance and reputation of their business.

This chapter will show you how to:

- Understand the different styles of communication that each of us can use in different situations
- Realize the importance of listening skills to help ensure that people feel that they are being heard
- Ensure that you choose the ideal form of communication for your purpose
- Ensure that meetings are necessary and well-run, with structured agendas and good chairing
- Deal with the challenges of managing virtual and remote teams where communication may be constrained
- Successfully manage a multicultural team and ensure that you have an optimal working culture.

You are a full-time communicator

'The single biggest problem in communication is the illusion that it has taken place.'
George Bernard Shaw

'To effectively communicate, we must realize that we are all different in the way we perceive the world and use this understanding as a guide to our communication with others.'
Anthony Robbins

How often in the day are you communicating with other people? Think about how you spend your working day and of all the different kinds of information, data, decisions and news you need to share with others in some form of communication:

- good news or bad news
- expected or unexpected
- straightforward or complicated
- for certain people only or for many
- to be told to others
- to be learnt from others
- to be shared
- to be discussed
- conclusions to be reached
- information to be combined
- gaps to be filled
- decisions to be made
- appreciation and thanks.

Some might say that when you are silently doing some work (e.g. testing some equipment or reading a manual), you are not communicating. But you are communicating something to those who observe you through your silent non-verbal communication.

I have come to the conclusion that everything you do as a manager is a form of communication. I am not suggesting that you are always wanting or needing to communicate but rather that other people will constantly receive all kinds of verbal and non-verbal messages from you. For example, the time you leave your office to go home is a form of communication – it shows others your work ethic and potentially suggests to others your expectations of how long people should stay in the office each day.

Communication styles

'She never listens to me and always shouts at me so loudly ... he always wants the last word ... she never clearly explained it to me ... my boss is so annoying and argumentative ... she always skim-reads everything I give her ... never likes to speak to me in person and always sends me requests by email ... she is so quiet and never speaks up even when you know she has something to say ... I do not understand what he wants us to do ... he jumps to conclusions and stops listening...'

Do such opinions and thoughts sound familiar?

A successful manager needs to create a working environment for his or her team where each team member clearly communicates any needed or necessary information, ideas and decisions to those individuals who need to know, and to have this information shared in such a way that it is received and understood by the other parties.

We are all unique and have developed our own communication styles and preferences, some of which may be positive and productive, while others might impact negatively upon the team. Some of us are extroverts, others very quiet; some like to write, others enjoy speaking in public; some are very loud and can seem aggressive, others speak too much.

What is your style like? Ask your team what they think of your style – what is good and what is not so good? What could be changed and improved?

The importance of listening skills

'I listen very well. I never interrupt. I never deflect the course of the conversation with a comment of my own. People, if you pay attention, change the direction of one another's conversations constantly. It's like having a passenger in your car who suddenly grabs the steering wheel and turns you down a side street.'

Garth Stein

The next time you are having a conversation with a group or an individual, observe how each of you communicates.

- Who is truly listening?
- How often are people interrupting each other?
- Is more than one person speaking at the same time?
- Is the flow of the discussion often being changed?
- Are people concentrating and paying attention?
- Is there a pause between people speaking?

I suspect you would not be impressed with what you observe, and I have come to realize that the biggest hurdle to good team performance is the failure to listen well to what others are trying to communicate.

Do people not listen to you? How do you feel about this? If we do not hear what the other person is trying to communicate, we face:

- demotivating and disengaging the other person
- wasting time and resources, because we may repeat things or miss opportunities or dangers
- failing to grow through learning from other people's ideas and points of view.

The complexity and information overload that we face in our 24/7 interconnected world, so full of noise and information, does not make listening easy but it does actually make it more essential that we listen well.

How can you be a team boss who listens effectively?

Pause and reflect before you speak and always remember a very useful abbreviation: W.A.I.T. This is to remind you of a very important question: *'Why am I talking?'. It* might encourage you to listen and observe more and speak less. After all, you have two ears and two eyes but only one mouth!

After someone has spoken to you, acknowledge that you have heard them before rushing to respond. Likewise, when responding to a written idea, comment or opinion, always try to show you have read and absorbed what has been shared with you before giving your own ideas etc.

Remember to be empathic and develop the mentality of wishing first to understand and then to be understood by others. I believe as a team head that it is sometimes better to really understand what your team is thinking and saying than to obsess over making sure they hear what you want them to hear.

Encourage your team to share their thoughts, opinions and ideas with you.

Discuss with the team your expectations of how the team should communicate between themselves and with other stakeholders. Also, ask them about their expectations.

Forms of communication

When you have some information to share with all of your team or with just one member, how do you decide the form of communication? Do you choose to:

- write a short or long email? Who do you copy the email to?
- write a memo or report?
- pick up the phone?
- arrange a video conference or Skype call?
- send a fax?
- speak face to face?
- call a formal or informal team meeting?
- send an SMS?
- post something on the company's social media pages?
- ask someone else to pass on your message?
- keep quiet and use non-verbal body language to pass on a message?
- do nothing, assuming the other person already knows?

Do you have preferred ways of communicating? Do you prefer emails, phone calls or meetings? Many things will influence your choice from the options: common sense, your working environment, working culture norms, the location of the other person, how urgent the matter is, the time of day, the type of job, the expectations of your boss or company etc.

Here is some advice to help you in your choice of communication.

- Keep it clear and concise.
- Indicate the urgency and importance of what you are communicating.
- Be ready to follow up (e.g. call after sending an urgent email).
- Be explicit about whether you are communicating in expectation of a reply, other action or simply to share some information.

I realize that some people prefer to write things down and others prefer to speak. No matter what your normal style is, be prepared to alter your style to ensure the greatest effectiveness, e.g. if you typically avoid calling people on the phone and only email, be ready to make a phone call when an email may not be appropriate (e.g. not urgent or personal enough).

Allow how you communicate to win over your staff and to motivate them to listen and to follow your lead. Be genuine and authentic. Show that you are thoughtful, that you care and that you are human.

Managing emails

How many emails have you received in your inbox so far today? So far this week? We all receive and send many emails and you might wish to set some guidelines with your team to ensure that they only send out emails that are appropriate and useful in helping you all to achieve your goals.

You might set team rules about:

- who you should typically 'cc' when writing emails
- which emails to reply to
- how long or short your emails should be.

Meetings

Meetings are a key aspect of leading a team. You may not enjoy spending hours in meetings but, like it or not, in many organizations they have become a key part of ensuring that teams can be successful. As a manager it is your role to ensure that any meetings you arrange with your team (and others) are appropriate and necessary as well as being well-organized and well-run.

The five secrets of successfully chairing and leading team meetings

> *'If you don't know where you are going, you will probably end up somewhere else.'*
>
> Lawrence Peter

1 Determine the desired outcomes and translate them into an agenda

Why do you need to hold a meeting? What are the desired outcomes you have in mind? It is important that you are clear about this before planning a meeting, and definitely before you share details of the meeting with your team.

- Do you need to share information about some plans? Is the desired outcome that all of the attendees should be given some specific plan of action, some specific knowledge etc?
- Do you need to have a debate or discussion and then to make a decision? Is the desired outcome that all the attendees are party to a decision?
- Do you need a meeting for team-building purposes, e.g. to bring the team together to share some common challenges and issues? Is the desired outcome a more aligned team?

The ideal agenda is a document that sets out the expectations of the meeting. It should include:

- issues and topics for discussion, each as a separate agenda item
- the names of who will present each issue or topic
- proposed timings, i.e. the time to be spent on each agenda item.

2 Decide who should attend and how they should prepare

On my training programmes, participants often complain about having to attend too many meetings where they feel their attendance is of no value and that they are wasting their time having to sit through hours of discussions. Have you ever had this feeling? If you or any of your team were not in a meeting, what more productive tasks could they be doing (this is the so-called 'opportunity cost' of attending the meeting)?

You might wish to have an entire group or team attend a meeting for reasons of team cohesion, common understanding, team unity etc. But if this is not the case, be selective about who should attend and for how long – people can be asked to attend only for specific agenda items to avoid taking up so much of their time.

You must also be careful not to burden your team with too much pre-meeting preparation – only ask of them what is really needed and important to ensure that the meeting can achieve its aims. Do you share in advance a detailed proposal which is to be voted on in the meeting without much time spent on discussion? Or do you share a short summary beforehand and use the meeting to present and discuss the proposal?

3 Plan the form and style of meeting professionally

Consider the nature of the meeting.

- Is it a regular meeting (e.g. monthly sales review meeting) or a special one-off meeting?
- Is it a formal meeting with an agenda and in which minutes will be taken, or is it an informal meeting?

Should the meeting be face to face or by video-conferencing or telephone? Or using software to allow information to be shared on each participants' computer screen. Should it be a meeting at which everyone stands rather than being seated? Is a meeting the best communication tool to achieve your desired outcomes? Sometimes an email or memo might suffice and would be less time-consuming and costly than a meeting, particularly if attendees must travel to the meeting location.

4 Chair the meeting like a great leader

> *'Effective chairing will ensure that a meeting achieves its aims and objectives. Chairs should facilitate, encourage, focus and clarify.'*
>
> University of Winchester (UK) website

If the meeting is one that you have organized, you will probably wish to lead and chair the meeting and your leadership skills will be put to the test.

Based on my experience, here are some tips on how to ensure that meetings you chair are successful.

- Understand the issues and information being discussed; you must at least read the preparation materials and come prepared.
- Allow everyone to express their opinions, do not talk too much yourself and do not allow anyone to ridicule or belittle another person's ideas and contribution.
- Keep the discussions on topic and on time and do not allow people to talk for the sake of it.
- Show respect for values, think of all attendees and do not criticize or try to push your own opinions too much – if you wish to impose your opinion, do not ask for others' opinions!
- If you wish to seek a decision from the group, through a vote or majority consensus, be sure you enable everyone to share their views.
- Try to keep the entire meeting positive and civil and as short as possible, and listen well to all that is shared as well as that which is not shared.

5 Have clear and actionable minutes

Minutes are a written record of the meeting and they should record the decisions made at the meeting, including details of who will action and follow up the decisions and actions agreed upon, and within what time frame. As with goal-setting, the actions required after a meeting must be clearly recorded and shared with all attendees to ensure no misunderstandings.

How to work with remotely located team members

Do you have team members who are located away from your office – perhaps in another town or even overseas? This is now common in our increasingly globalized world. You may also have a virtual team under your leadership, with members scattered around the world and only coming together for specific reasons (see the project teams section later in this chapter).

If you have a remotely located team member or members, you will need to work out how to maintain communication, sharing and general interaction. This can be a real challenge if the person cannot easily attend team meetings or just walk into your office or grab you for coffee to discuss something informally.

In such cases you may need to make an extra effort to connect with the team member, e.g. arranging weekly video-conference catch-ups.

Managing a multicultural team

Another challenge arises when you have team members who come from different cultures. The different cultures might be ethnic, religious, geographic or the working culture of an employee's former company.

As a team leader your role is to:

- ensure that anyone joining you from a different culture is able to fit in and settle into your team without negatively disrupting your working culture and norms
- identify and appreciate the cultural differences within your team and work with your multicultural mix
- educate the rest of your team about accepting diversity, helping them to understand that just because someone thinks or acts differently, that does not make them wrong or a poor performer.

The following are examples of cultural differences that you might experience with staff from different parts of the world.

Some people:	Whereas others:
Do not question authority (e.g. their bosses)	Would actively question and challenge
Work best through informal structures	Need formal rules and processes
Are individualistic and want their own success	Like being in groups and having group success
Are interested in people and connections	Focus on systems, procedures, products etc
Are material and focused on remuneration	Care about quality of life and well-being

Are happy to work long hours without breaks	Need a formal lunchtime and go home on time
Keep quiet and do not rush to give opinions	Never seem to keep quiet and always share

If you would like to delve deeper into this subject, look at the work on workplace culture by Hofstede and Trompenaars.

Leading temporary, short-term or project teams

Sometimes teams are created that will have only a short lifespan, perhaps working on a short project that will last only a few weeks or months. Leading such teams presents the following challenges.

- The team members may never have worked together before.
- They may have never worked with you before.
- There may be little time to become familiar with one another.
- High performance may be expected immediately.
- There may be no budget and no time for team bonding or team building.
- The work might be stressful as there may never be enough time and manpower to do everything that needs doing.

The key to success in such a situation is for a manager to show in an open and honest way that he or she understands the team's challenges and issues, and that together the team will seek ways of ensuring that they achieve their goals without getting burnt-out.

I have recently been working with a project team that faced all of the above issues. With coaching, the team's manager worked very hard to ensure that the team could be aligned with common expectations and she made sure that they regularly socialized together. Each week she would also have a short team meeting where she would explore how the team members were feeling, connecting and communicating together. Topics such as stress, overwork and pressure were discussed and the team members learnt to try to help each other. The team was very successful in completing its project and the team's manager was highly rated by her staff and company.

Summary

This chapter has shown you all of the communication issues that a successful manager must master to ensure that they can create and maintain a high-performing team.

You now understand that communication is a full-time role; today, a manager who remained holed up in their office without speaking with their staff would be very lucky to keep their job!

You appreciate each person's communication style and realize that listening is the main communication style for any high-performing team leader.

You can choose the ideal form of communication for use in different situations.

You are able to organize and chair all kinds of team meetings, including those involving remotely located staff.

You understand the challenges of working with short-term or project teams where you lack time to create an ideal team working environment.

SUNDAY
MONDAY
TUESDAY
WEDNESDAY
THURSDAY
FRIDAY
SATURDAY

Fact-check (answers at the back)

1. What does W.A.I.T. stand for?
   a) Why am I thinking? ❑
   b) Why am I talking? ❑
   c) Wait, act, indicate and talk ❑
   d) None of the above ❑

2. An ideal team meeting agenda should include:
   a) Issues and topics for discussion ❑
   b) Names of who will present each topic ❑
   c) Proposed time to be spent on each topic ❑
   d) All of the above ❑

3. Which of the following might influence your choice of the form of communication?
   a) The expectations of your boss or company ❑
   b) The location of the other person ❑
   c) How urgent the matter is ❑
   d) All of the above ❑

4. A workplace culture is:
   a) The habits of the group ❑
   b) The thinking and norms of the group ❑
   c) The behaviours and styles of the group ❑
   d) All of the above ❑

5. Ideal communication should be viewed as:
   a) A minor part of your role ❑
   b) A full-time task ❑
   c) Left to your team ❑
   d) None of the above ❑

6. Which of the following is *not* the trait of a good listener?
   a) An empathic person ❑
   b) Seeks to understand rather than be understood ❑
   c) Tries to speak first in meetings ❑
   d) Acknowledges what others say ❑

7. In a meeting, what should you do when someone else is speaking?
   a) Interrupt them ❑
   b) Not listen ❑
   c) Think of what you want to say ❑
   d) Listen to them and then acknowledge what they have shared ❑

8. How should you manage your emails?
   a) Decide who you should typically copy emails to ❑
   b) Decide which emails to reply to ❑
   c) Decide how long or short your emails should be ❑
   d) All of the above ❑

9. Which of the following is a problem of working with remotely located team members?
   a) They may be from another culture ❑
   b) You cannot easily meet them face to face ❑
   c) You cannot easily see what they are doing ❑
   d) All of the above ❑

10. Which of the following is *not* one of the secrets of holding successful meetings?

a) Invite as many people as possible to attend ❏

b) Determine the required outcomes ❏

c) Set a clear agenda with topics for discussion ❏

d) Chair the meeting well ❏

THURSDAY

Managing poor performers in your team

Managing staff who are not working and performing to the optimum can be your most difficult task and is the topic I am most asked about in my coaching and training work, regardless of whereabouts in the world my clients are located.

This chapter will show you the typical performance issues that you might face and how to think through your response to different situations. Each challenge will be unique and you will need to find a suitable response for the precise circumstances of each case.

This chapter will show you how to:

- Explore what performance problems can look like and learn how to understand the possible causes of poor or underperformance
- Explore the team performance issues associated with older as well as younger staff
- Recognize the problems that toxic people can create within a team
- Understand that performance issues can be caused by the entire team rather than by an individual's problems
- Understand each person's different decision-making styles and how these can impact upon a team's performance
- Ensure that 'groupthink' is not occurring
- Give and receive feedback to help to improve your team's performance.

What does poor or underperformance look like?

'If you have a job without aggravation, you don't have a job.'

Malcolm Forbes

Members of your team can fail to meet targets and goals that you have set for them. They can also have a negative effect on others in the team which might affect the performance of other team members or their willingness to stay in your team.

How can you spot team members with potential performance issues *before* the problems manifest themselves in goals not being achieved? This would give you a chance to rectify things before it is too late. Here are some key questions to help you spot who may have performance issues.

- Who complains and gossips?
- Who seems to create conflict and is argumentative?
- Who is acting selfishly and not sharing?
- Who answers back, and does not seem to respect or listen to you?
- Who in your team do other team members not like to work or communicate with?
- Who seems to be lazy and often absent or having long coffee breaks?
- Who never seems to start or finish their work on time?
- Who often asks for help and says they do not understand what you have already told them?

Possible causes of poor or underperformance

It is important as a manager to seek out the root causes of why someone is not working and performing to the optimum in your team. Sometimes what you see is only a symptom of some underlying issue. For example, Person A acts lazily and spends his time gossiping and complaining rather than focusing on his work. The possible causes might be a combination of:

● not having clear objectives or goals
● not having the tools to complete his work
● not being incentivized or motivated
● not having the skills or knowledge to know what to do
● being bored by their work
● being afraid of making a mistake.

It is not enough to simply stop the person complaining and gossiping. It is your task to find out what is happening and to try to help solve the underlying issues. Sometimes a few performance issues are linked and you need to tackle a few things to arrive at the root cause. The diagram below shows how one problem (Issue 4) has underlying causes, the key one being that the person is not interested in their work (Issue 1).

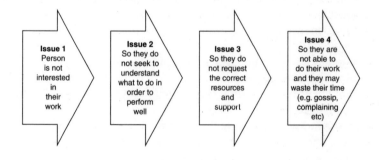

Often, such flows become downward spirals. In the scenario above, the person is likely to lose interest even more if they are not in a position to do their work well.

A very useful framework for seeking the reasons for performance issues (and one which complements the six-step model in Tuesday's chapter), is the widely used Gilbert's Six Boxes, where any reason for an individual's poor performance would fall into one or more of the following six 'buckets':

Necessary feedback and expectations	Needed resources available	Appropriate incentives
Required knowledge and skills	Optimal ability to do work	Attitude and motivations

The top three boxes relate more to what you and the organization needs to provide and do, while the bottom three relate more to the individual.

Based on these six boxes, explore the reasons for any performance issues in your team by asking yourself these six sets of questions.

1 Do I need to give the individual or individuals feedback to help them improve their performance? How strong or firm do I need to be? Have I neglected to do so? How can I alter my communication and leadership style to help?
2 Is the individual lacking anything in terms of resources (support, information from other sources, equipment and time) that they need to perform better? Are the goals and direction not ideal or not clearly stated and communicated?
3 Is the individual correctly incentivized to perform better? What kinds of incentives or motivators are missing or not aligned with the required performance?
4 What knowledge, experience or skills is the individual lacking or misusing that is affecting their performance? How can I solve this?
5 Is the individual really suited to the work and tasks that they have been given? Are they able to succeed in their role if given help or have they reached a ceiling?
6 In what ways is the individual not motivated to perform well? What factors are holding them back and demotivating them?

Is it a team-wide performance problem?

If one of your team has an issue, be careful about jumping to conclusions and assuming that it is just that individual's problem. It could be that this individual is reacting to problems within the whole team, e.g. others not sharing information with him or her.

Is the team stuck in the 'storming' phase (remember Tuckman's model from the Sunday chapter) so the team's performance has declined? The graph below is a reminder of the development stages of a team and how teams can fall back into the storming phase.

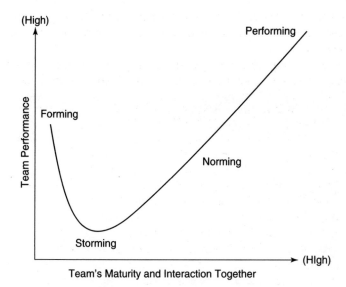

Beware of individuals blaming others

Some individuals may try to blame others in the team or to blame you for their poor performance, even when it appears clear to you that it is the individual who is at fault. You need to know your team well and to able to observe what is really happening, which is something that becomes easier with time and experience. If you initially blame the wrong party or reason for a performance problem, be ready to apologize and be open with those involved. We all value honesty and humility in those we work with. People can be very forgiving even if falsely accused of something.

If ever in doubt, pause and take a calm step back. Look for the bigger picture, what is sometimes referred to as a 'balcony' or 'helicopter' view, of what is happening.

Giving feedback to your team

When coaching individuals I often hear comments such as: 'But no one ever told me that I was not performing well ... I did not realize that my boss was not happy with my performance until the day he fired me.'

It is not enough simply to give your team goals and objectives; it is essential that you provide excellent feedback which forms part of your evaluation of their performance. Too often, managers only give feedback at the time of the company's annual performance appraisal review. At other times there is typically no structured sharing and communication.

Here are some key dos and don'ts about how you should give feedback.

- You should remember to give feedback as often as possible about all the good work that your team members are doing and not give feedback only when there is a problem.
- Feedback should be timely and should be given immediately after the performance issue has occurred.
- Feedback should be as clear and specific as possible, and you should give your own opinion rather than quoting what others might think.
- Try to describe what you observe about the person's performance, not simply making accusations or judgements.
- Always try to give positive feedback first before moving on to any potentially critical or negative areas of discussion.
- Allow the person to listen and to respond.

'I praise loudly. I blame softly.'
Catherine the Great

Teach your team to receive feedback and overcome blind spots

It is not enough to give feedback; your team members need to be encouraged to hear and to listen well, so learn to share with them. Tell them that they do not need to immediately respond and try to justify everything that is being discussed about their performance.

Sometimes team members may have difficulty hearing and agreeing with your feedback because they do not believe or accept that they might have a particular weakness. This could be called the individual's blindspot and you need to encourage them to be open-minded and understand that we all have weaknesses and issues that we may not be aware of but which others are.

Types of performance issues

Here are some of the common people issues that you are likely to face when you start managing a team.

Older, long-serving staff

Often there is no problem in working with older and long-serving people, and their knowledge, experience and wisdom can really help you and the rest of the team. However, sometimes older staff may not be willing to listen and work with you, particularly if you are introducing new ideas and changes. Such people can be negative and cynical, and will often speak slightingly about what you are trying to do and will appear to undermine you.

How can you work with and manage such people?

- Were they so used to a previous management style that now they are not willing to adjust to your leadership? Perhaps initially you can give them some leeway and time, but you need to set clear expectations and be ready to be firm.
- They may feel that they know how to do your job better than you do. This is never easy to deal with but you must not let them undermine you.

- They may feel threatened by the changes you appear to represent and they may fear for their jobs. Try to win them over and reassure them.
- Do they resent you being appointed as their manager because one of them was passed over for the role? By slowly trying to gain their respect you can hope to win them over.
- Are they unable to understand or do what you are asking of them? Perhaps extra sharing, communication or training is required.
- You may need to be firm and ask them to stop being negative or speaking unpleasantly about you. A point may be reached where you will need to give warning letters and threaten to dismiss someone. You will need to make sure that you have kept your boss informed along the way and also sought advice about employment law from your human resources team.

Generation Y staff

You may need to hire staff aged in their twenties, part of the so-called Generation Y. This age group brings with them expectations that can create problems; these include wanting responsibility immediately, not wanting to work long hours, wanting to be promoted quickly and not connecting well with older staff in the team.

How can you ensure such young people succeed in your team?

- Teach and show them what is expected of them in their work and be open with them about the realities of how much responsibility you can give them and of the probable timings of future promotion.
- Spend time understanding their motivations and expectations.
- Guide and mentor them, encouraging them to accept what needs to be done in their jobs and careers.
- Be ready to be firm if they are not adjusting to what is expected of them.
- Be aware that younger people may not be as loyal as older staff so they might resign if they feel you are pushing them too much or if the work (in their opinion) is boring or not challenging enough. In Friday's chapter we cover the topic of staff retention.

Bad examples

You are likely to have at least one team member who may be setting a bad and unacceptable example to the rest of the team, and you will need to intervene in some way. What could someone do that is unacceptable? Here are some examples I have come across:

● often being late for work
● spending too long away from their desk
● being slow and lazy
● being selfish and not sharing
● preventing other people from doing their work
● not listening to what you are communicating
● not doing as they are asked
● being dishonest and lying
● speaking unpleasantly about other people
● criticizing you and/or the organization
● openly talking about leaving
● not being willing to learn new things.

Dealing with unacceptable behaviour

Here is a three-step approach to follow.

1 **Find out why**
Explore the underlying reasons for the individual's behaviour; typically this is linked to the individual's motivations, attitudes, behaviours and values. Gather feedback from other people (while also responding to people's complaints about the individual's actions).

2 **Agree a plan**
Have a meeting with the individual. Ideally this should be a face-to-face confidential meeting – although your boss or human resources manager may need to be present – in which you explain your concerns in detail.
   – Listen to the responses and opinions of the individual.
   – Be ready to explain again why there is a problem, if necessary talking about the organization's values and culture.

- Try to agree a written action plan of required changes and a time frame for improved performance.
- Warn the person of the consequences of not changing their behaviour.
- Agree when you will meet again, if this is appropriate.

3 Follow up and monitor the individual

Follow up and monitor the individual's performance. Give the individual feedback, letting them know what changes you are observing. If the changes are not positive, you will need to consider disciplinary action, including giving warning letters as well as considering dismissal, in line with your company's rules and your country's employment laws and regulations.

Dealing with a high performer with negative issues

Sometimes negative behaviour is exhibited by someone who is achieving their goals and objectives and who may be viewed as a high-performing member of the team. This can create a dilemma for you as you will probably not wish to lose such a person. From my experience, I would strongly encourage you to:

SUNDAY

MONDAY

TUESDAY

WEDNESDAY

THURSDAY

FRIDAY

SATURDAY

- talk with the individual openly, sharing your concerns about their attitude and behaviour. Do not keep quiet for fear of losing them.
- consider disciplinary action and even dismissal if the individual will not acknowledge their need to improve and will not change how they are acting. You cannot keep such a 'toxic' person in a team without negatively affecting the entire team.
- explain to the team what led to a person's dismissal – this will counter any inaccurate gossip or rumours.

Letting such a person go will demonstrate to the rest of the team that you are serious about creating and maintaining an ideal working environment and culture based on certain values. Such firm action is all part of creating a culture of excellence – this is explored in more detail in the Saturday chapter.

Poor decision-makers

ALL RIGHT, THEN – LET'S HAVE A DISCUSSION ABOUT WHETHER TO HAVE A DISCUSSION

Humans are creatures of habit and we can become lazy about thinking through everything that we do in our work. How does your team deal with and think through problems and solutions in its daily work?

- Do some members always seem to jump to one conclusion or idea and refuse to listen to other ideas?
- Do others float various solutions and never seem to agree which is the ideal way forward?

- Do team members seem to follow the same style in every interaction you have with them?
- What are your own decision-making habits?

According to Ken Brousseau's famous decision-making model, optimal decision-making in any given situation revolves around two questions.

1 How much information should ideally be analysed in making a decision?
2 How many ideas and solutions need to be optimally considered before a final decision can be made?

Your challenge is ensure that you teach your team to think well and to make correct decisions. Make sure that they avoid making the following common mistakes:

- using too little information or ignoring information
- being overwhelmed by too much information
- jumping at the first solution or idea that is suggested and not looking any further
- implementing someone else's suggestion without thinking it through sufficiently.

You must also be ready to review their work and provide feedback and advice when they may be going astray in their decision-making.

- Sometimes you can leave your team to make mistakes, allowing them to learn from such mistakes.
- At other times, the potential mistake might be too costly and you must guide them to another solution, explaining to them your rationale and logic.

Avoiding the problem of 'groupthink'

Sometimes a group jumps to collective decisions and conclusions which may prove to be wrong and lead to performance problems. 'Groupthink' occurs when a team discusses an issue and agrees on a way forward while ignoring lone voices that may have other suggestions to make.

This is a common problem within teams where there is a culture of not speaking up and of not questioning what others are saying. In certain cultures, if a team leader makes a suggestion, it is highly likely that the group will support it and will ignore other ideas. This can be very dangerous. As well as leading to potentially wrong decisions being made, it can also be very demotivating to those in your team, particularly those who are creative and innovative, who may feel they are not being listened to.

Are you the cause of the problem?

In what ways might you be directly contributing to the poor performance of your team members?

- Are you delaying any decisions or communication, e.g. a difficult conversation with a poor performer?
- Are you ignoring what is in front of you, e.g. are you reluctant to admit that someone in your team is at fault or not being a good team player?
- Are you biased in some way, e.g. always favouring certain members of your team and being blind to their weaknesses?
- Are there any trust issues involved? Are people in your team reluctant to share with you their ideas and concerns? Do they not trust that you will use what they share in a fair and objective way (i.e. do they fear you will use it against them)?

One solution is to build up as much trust and rapport with your team as possible. As you grow your management career, do 'walk the talk', ensuring that what you think, what you say and what you do are all in visible alignment.

Remember that as the head of the team, you are ultimately responsible for the entire team's performance. You cannot ever say that it was not your fault if your team performs badly!

Summary

This chapter has been a guide to the thinking and solutions that can help you to understand and solve poor performance problems that might arise in your team.

You are now able to understand the kinds of possible performance problems that you may face.

You can use the Six Boxes questions to discover the possible reasons for team members' problems.

You know that there are some common patterns of poor performance, particularly when you have some older, more experienced staff or younger Generation Y staff in your team.

You know that sometimes problems that may appear to come from one or two individuals might actually be a team-wide issue.

You understand the ideal decision-making process and why poor decision-making might lead to poor performance.

SUNDAY

MONDAY

TUESDAY

WEDNESDAY

THURSDAY

FRIDAY

SATURDAY

Fact-check (answers at the back)

1. Which of the following is *not* one of the Six Boxes model?
   a) Needed resources available ❑
   b) Amount of holidays given ❑
   c) Optimal ability to do work ❑
   d) Attitude and motivations ❑

2. Which of the following could be viewed as unacceptable behaviour?
   a) Often being late for work ❑
   b) Spending too long away from desk ❑
   c) Being slow and lazy ❑
   d) All of the above ❑

3. How should you respond to anyone exhibiting unacceptable behaviour?
   a) Find out why ❑
   b) Agree a plan with the individual ❑
   c) Follow up and mentor the individual ❑
   d) All of the above ❑

4. A team-wide performance problem suggests the team is in which stage of the Tuckman model?
   a) Norming ❑
   b) Performing ❑
   c) Forming ❑
   d) Storming ❑

5. Why might older staff cause performance issues?
   a) Fear of change ❑
   b) Thinking they know more than you ❑
   c) Jealousy over your appointment as manager ❑
   d) All of above ❑

6. Good feedback should be:
   a) Clear and timely ❑
   b) Only in writing ❑
   c) Given only over phone ❑
   d) Given only at end of year ❑

7. What is 'groupthink'?
   a) People have different ideas ❑
   b) People agree to one idea too easily and quickly ❑
   c) People never agree ❑
   d) It is what your boss thinks ❑

8. Why should we not jump to conclusions when investigating a performance issue?
   a) The causes may not be what you initially think or see ❑
   b) There may be more than one reason ❑
   c) It might be a team-wide issue or an individual's issue ❑
   d) All of above ❑

9. Which of the following is a common mistake when making decisions?
   a) Using too little information ❑
   b) Ignoring information ❑
   c) Jumping at the first solution or idea that is suggested ❑
   d) All of the above ❑

10. Which of the following is the ideal way to receive feedback?
    a) Listening well ❑
    b) Not rushing to speak ❑
    c) Not feeling compelled to justify what you are being told ❑
    d) All of the above ❑

FRIDAY

Managing high performers in your team

Having created and built up a team, you need to ensure that you encourage and manage those in your team who are performing well and maximize the chances of them performing even better in the future. You will also need to ensure that you retain and keep these high performers.

This chapter will help you to:

- Understand who in your team is performing well and who has the potential to perform even better in the future
- Differentiate between those in your team who are performing well and those who are not, objectively measuring your team members' performance
- Rank your team members by their performance and by their potential
- Deal with high-performing staff who may not be exhibiting the values, behaviour and attitudes that you expect of them
- Be an excellent situational leader, adapting your management style as needed, and balancing how directive and how supportive you need to be
- Understand the importance of retaining key staff and having a talent retention strategy
- Create a strategy based around the six secrets of retaining high-performing staff.

Who is performing well in your team?

> *'Teamwork is so important that it is virtually impossible for you to reach the heights of your capabilities or make the money that you want without becoming very good at it.'*
>
> Brian Tracy

How many of your team are performing well? Who is outstanding? Which of your team has the potential to perform even better in the future?

Each organization has its own model for monitoring and evaluating its employees' performance. Do you know and understand your own organization's model? Typically there would be a combination of:

- setting performance goals, and also goals based on certain soft skills and values
- creating a timetable for discussing and evaluating the achievement of the goals
- having a series of discussions between each employee and his or her line manager to evaluate the actual performance of the employee, with most organizations grading their staff based on:
  - achievement of their work goals
  - how well the individual reflects certain values or core competencies.

Differentiating among your team

Many managers have difficulty in being honest and open with all members of their team about each team member's performance and potential. Why is this so? It is because some managers find it hard to tell some of their team that they are not performing well, fearing that it would upset them and demotivate them. As a result, a manager might give similar performance rankings or gradings to their team members. However, by not being honest and differentiating between different levels of performance, you may demotivate your better performers because they feel that you are not valuing their hard work and good performance.

Some organizations insist upon what is called 'forced ranking', which was first popularized by General Electric. With forced ranking, a manager must give a range of performance gradings to their team members based on certain percentages. A typical example might be as follows.

Typical grades	Typical grading definitions	Example percentage of staff to be given each grade
A	Excellent	10%
B	Good	35%
C	Average	35%
D	Below average	10%
E	Not performing	10%

In this example, you would only be able to give one in ten of your team an 'excellent' grading.

You must learn to be very objective in grading your team members and in giving them feedback on their performance. Keep notes about how you arrive at each of your team member's gradings and be ready to justify your decisions to others. It is important that you are seen by your team to be fair, understanding and objective.

Performance versus potential

Some of your team might have performed well in the year to date, but how do you know if they will continue working well and whether they could take on more work and responsibilities in the future? In other words, do they have a high potential to grow in your team in your organization?

How would you define potential with your team members?

- To keep performing well in their current role with their existing goals?
- To be able to grow and take on more responsibilities, and possibly be promoted into a more senior role?
- To be able to consistently live by and demonstrate your team's values and core competencies?
- The degree to which they want to take on more responsibility?

It can be easy to communicate what you think of their potential to a team member with high potential – they would be only too happy to be told that you think they have great potential to grow and succeed in your team and in your organization. Your difficulty comes in telling someone with limited potential what you think of them. As with poor performers, the best practice is that you must be honest, but diplomatic!

I would encourage you to use a table such as the one shown below to rank your team members in terms of *both* their performance and their potential.

Potential (in future)	High	Low performers with high potential		High performers with high potential
	Medium			
	Low	Low performers with low potential		High performers with low potential
		Low	Medium	High
		Performance (to date)		

How would you lead your team members depending on their performance and potential rankings? As you gain more experience of managing teams, you will develop your own style of working with each team member, but here are some ideas to get you started:

High performers with high potential

These are the stars of your team and you should make sure that you retain and support them. Retaining such high performers is a key role of any successful manager. It is also important that you do not let their success go to their heads and they must be encouraged to be good team players, helping the entire team to succeed. These issues are discussed in more detail later in this chapter.

High performers with low potential
They may have peaked and reached their maximum potential in their current role. Are they comfortable being thought of as having low potential with limited promotion possibilities? You could try to retain them in their current role in which they are performing well.

Low performers with high potential
Why are they currently underperforming? Would they be able to perform better in a different role or even in a different team? The key is to try to create a role for them in which they can flourish and perform well.

Low performers with low potential
Are you able to develop and grow such team members? If they have been performing poorly and also have poor potential to perform well in the future, then it is possible that you will need to let these staff go to make room for better performing people.

Individuals with average or medium levels of performance and/or potential

Only you can decide how you work with and manage such individuals, who are often referred to as the 'backbone' of a team. It would be unusual to have a team without such members and your task is to work to improve both their current performance and also their future potential.

But be careful not to push all of your staff to improve; some people are genuinely happy to remain 'average' performers and do not have the desire and ambition to be pushed to perform better or to improve their perceived potential.

Performing well, but...

Have you ever known someone who performs well (in terms of achieving their goals) but they may not be someone you wish to work with? For instance, they might be sexist, lazy, arrogant, deceptive, not communicate well, not listen, be selfish etc.

You will at some point have team members who are achieving their goals and are deemed to be high performers, but they may have some attitude and behaviour problems and are not exhibiting the expected values of your team. This will be a challenging situation for you. On the matrix below, people like this would sit towards the bottom right; as a manager, you need to try to move them to the top right corner (shown by the arrow).

		Low	Medium	High
In line with values expected	Exceeding			
	Meeting			
	Below			High performing staff with behaviour and attitude Issues
		Individuals' performance		

How can you do this?

- Have you spoken with the individual in question to discuss your concerns? You need to do so, and during such a conversation try to discover whether the individual agrees with your opinion. Ask them why they are acting this way.
- Are they demotivating others in your team and organization? You may hear complaints from others.
- How willing and able are you to try to change their unacceptable behaviour(s)? You must decide how firm you will need to be and choose how you will manage them – see the section below on being a situational leader.
- 'To keep or not to keep them?' Are you afraid of losing them from your team if you push them too hard to change? You will need to understand how difficult it would be to replace such an individual with an equally strong performer.

A high performer whose performance declines

You may have to deal with a high performer whose performance is starting to decline. If you view the decline as a temporary blip, you might not enter into much discussion with the individual. However, if it is not a temporary decline, you need to investigate the cause(s). There might be a number of factors involved, such as:

- boredom with their work
- loss of interest in their work
- not getting on with you as their manager.

To help get such a good performer back on track, you will need to be a good situational leader.

Situational leadership

Would you manage a high performer in the same way that you manage a poorly performing member of your team? Do you ever consciously alter your management style depending on the situation and the person you are talking about?

Being able to alter your management style to the circumstances is a key skill of a top performing team leader. Ken Blanchard's Situational Leadership model, shown below, is a good demonstration of why this is so important.

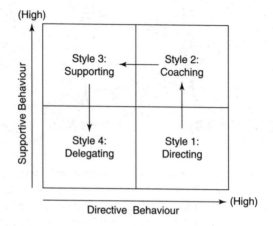

With any member of your team, you can choose to be a combination of:

- **directive** – telling and showing a person in your team what they have to do and then closely supervising their performance
- **supportive** – actively providing guidance, feedback and support to a person when they are working under you and encouraging them.

The Situational Leadership model shows four possible management styles that you could adopt in any given situation. Each is explained below, with an indication of when each style might be appropriate.

Style 1: Directing

This is sometimes called a 'I will decide what you do' style and is a style of offering a little support while being very directive. You would come across as being very decisive and clear.

WOULD YOU LIKE ME TO GIVE YOU A LITTLE PUSH?

You would normally use such a management style with new staff or with staff who have some serious performance issues. In both cases you need to explain clearly what needs to be done or achieved. It is a useful style when you have no time to allow the individual to learn for themselves what they need to do or to change. Be careful not to overuse this style, though, as it can be viewed as being too strong and could be seen as micro-managing.

Style 2: Coaching
This is sometimes called a 'Let's talk and I will decide' style. It is a style of being very engaged or involved with an individual in your team, and being both very decisive and very supportive.

This style is typically used when you need to be very actively involved in helping someone to achieve their goals and to improve their performance. An underperforming but established member of your team might need to be managed in this very hands-on way. If you manage someone in this way for too long, however, they might feel micro-managed and unable to make their own decisions.

Style 3: Supporting
This can be called a 'Let's talk and we both decide' style. It is still quite a hands-on style, where you feel you do not

have to be directive but still need to provide a lot of feedback, discussion and support.

Typically this style is used with staff who are experienced but still need active support and help. They do not need or expect you to direct them but still need your active support and involvement.

Style 4: Delegating
This can be called a 'Why don't you decide?' style. It is a style of offering very little directive and supportive support. It does not mean that you are not managing someone, but it does mean that you are not having to provide a hands-on and involved style and as a result you are giving an individual a lot of space in which to work and perform.

This is the ideal style that can be adopted with high-performing staff who know what they have to do and require less of your time compared to new staff or underperforming staff.

The three arrows in the diagram show the ideal flow in how you would change your style of managing an individual over time – from when they join your team (Style 1) to when they become a consistently high performer (Style 4).

I encourage you to start being very conscious of how you manage and communicate with each of your team. Decide if your style is optimal in each case, remembering to adjust your style as needed.

Retaining top performers

Having identified your top performers as well as those who have high potential, you must decide how you ensure that you retain such individuals and keep them in your team.

A good manager needs a talent retention strategy for those team members they wish to retain. The strategy can be quite simple and could start with answers to two questions:

1 Why do your staff choose to stay and work in your team?
2 What do they seek in their job, career and workplace?

These two questions link to discussions elsewhere in this book about employee motivation, and I would encourage you to ask your staff for their opinions in the form of an employee satisfaction survey. Ideally this should be anonymous so that your team are more comfortable with sharing and being honest. Such surveys can be very helpful in revealing what your team members really feel and think about:

● their work
● being in your team
● being managed by you.

Do not be offended if they surprise you by being critical and a little negative – it is better to know the truth than to be left in the dark thinking everything is fine. Facts are friendly, and once you know the truth you can act upon it.

Six secrets of retaining key staff

Here are six key areas that you could focus on as part of your talent retention strategy.

1 Be a leader that team members trust and want to work with
Communicate well with your team and, most importantly, listen to them. Ensure that you meet their expectations and when you cannot meet them, have an honest and open discussion about why not. I would add that you must 'walk the talk' and make sure that you do what you promise.

Also, do develop your leadership styles to inspire and motivate your team – the Saturday chapter explores this in more detail.

2 Reward team members fairly

Make sure that your team's remuneration model (including bonus and commission structures, salary review processes etc) is fair, open and transparent, while also ensuring that you pay your staff at competitive market levels. Humans like to compare things with others, so it is imperative that you show no favouritism or lack of objectivity in how each person in your team is evaluated, judged and rewarded.

3 Support team members' career and life plans

Understand what your team members' ambitions and career goals are and try to work with them in achieving their dreams. Part of this involves having a good succession planning model so that high performers can be groomed for more significant roles and can be promoted. Another aspect involves you having honest and open dialogue about what job opportunities may exist in your team or in the wider organization, and supporting your team members in moving to new roles. This may mean you have to let them join another team in your organization to give them the needed career growth.

4 Give team members work that they enjoy

Make sure that you try to match the work roles given to each of your team members with what they would like and enjoy doing. It is also advisable not to let your staff overwork and become burnt-out; they may enjoy what they do, but you must support them in having a good work–life balance.

5 Recognize team members' good work and efforts

How often do you say: 'Thank you', 'Well done', 'Good work' or 'Great performance'? When did you last publicly acknowledge the good work of members of your team? Remember that humans yearn for and need to be recognized. If in doubt, do not keep silent.

6 Create and maintain a positive environment

Try to ensure that within your team there is a healthy and open culture with no tension, anxiety, undue stress, negative gossip and rumours. You need your staff to be happy to come to work.

In my experience, following these six secrets will keep members of your team motivated and wanting to continue working with you.

Summary

This chapter has shown you how to successfully work with and retain your high-performing and high-potential staff.

You are now able to define who in your team is high-performing, understanding the importance of differentiating between those in your team who are performing well and those who are not.

You can analyse your team members by both their performance and by their potential.

You understand how to think through why your high-performing staff may have some behaviour or attitude issues and are not living up to the values expected of them.

You can vary your leadership style depending on the situation and on which of your team members you are communicating with and trying to manage.

You understand how to successfully retain your high-performing talent to ensure that you do not lose them to the competition.

SUNDAY
MONDAY
TUESDAY
WEDNESDAY
THURSDAY
FRIDAY
SATURDAY

Fact-check (answers at the back)

1. Which of the following is *not* one of the six retention secrets?
a) Being a good leader ❏
b) Firing staff who do not listen well ❏
c) Rewarding staff well ❏
d) Helping your staff to plan their careers ❏

2. Situational leadership involves:
a) Varying the style of management ❏
b) Being directive at times ❏
c) Being supportive at times ❏
d) All of the above ❏

3. In the situational leadership model, coaching is being:
a) High in directive and low in supportive styles ❏
b) High in both directive and supportive styles ❏
c) Low in both directive and supportive styles ❏
d) None of the above ❏

4. Why is a talent retention strategy important?
a) Losing staff is costly and disruptive ❏
b) Good talent is hard to replace ❏
c) It's not easy to keep your staff ❏
d) All of the above ❏

5. Why is it important to say 'Thank you' and 'Well done' to your staff?
a) It makes them feel valued ❏
b) It makes them feel that they have been recognized ❏
c) Both of the above. ❏
d) None of the above ❏

6. Which is it better to have in your team?
a) A high performer who is not in alignment with your company values ❏
b) A high performer who is in alignment with your company values ❏
c) A low performer with low potential ❏
d) A potentially high performer who is not in alignment with your values ❏

7. Why is it key to give your staff work that they enjoy?
a) They will be more successful ❏
b) They will burn out ❏
c) They will have no work–life balance ❏
d) None of the above ❏

8. Being a leader that others trust can help you to:
a) Retain your staff ❏
b) Motivate your staff ❏
c) Lead to better performance by your team ❏
d) All of the above ❏

9. Which is the ideal style of managing a team member who is experienced and high-performing?
a) Delegating style ❏
b) Coaching style ❏
c) Directive style ❏
d) Supportive style ❏

10. The 'I will decide what you do' style in the situational leadership model is the

a) Delegating style ❏
b) Coaching style ❏
c) Supportive style ❏
d) Directive style ❏

SUNDAY

MONDAY

TUESDAY

WEDNESDAY

THURSDAY

FRIDAY

SATURDAY

SATURDAY

Creating and maintaining a culture of excellence

It is not difficult to learn how to manage a team so that it performs to an acceptable level. But to lead a team to a level of performance that makes other people say: 'Wow, what a brilliant and amazing team!' is a little harder.

This chapter will help you to understand what you can do to raise your team members to a level of excellent performance combined with excellent potential. In terms of your role as manager, this chapter will help to elevate you from being a good team manager to one who is truly outstanding and admired.

This chapter will show you:

- What a culture of excellence is and why it worth aspiring to create such a culture in your team
- The seven key understandings that are the foundation for creating a culture of excellence within your team

What is a culture of excellence?

Any team, consciously or unconsciously, agrees a set of understandings around which all of its thinking and activities are organized. This is your team's culture.

What are your team's understandings? Are they optimal? Ideally, such understandings should be centred on achieving and maintaining excellence in all aspects of the team's work and workings.

I think the most helpful definition of excellence is optimizing the 'what we do' with the 'how we do it', i.e. choosing to do the optimal tasks and actions while also ensuring that such work is completed optimally. The diagram below shows this pictorially. Which box would you define as excellence?

What tasks and actions Does your team undertake?	Right ones	Doing the right things badly	Doing the right things well
	Wrong ones	Doing the wrong things badly	Doing the wrong things well
		Not well / Badly	Well
		How does your team perform its tasks and actions?	

Hopefully, you chose the top right-hand box! This is the correct answer: where your team are doing the right things well.

Note that understandings are linked to your team's written and unwritten goals, objectives, rules, norms, stated values and the content of your team charter (covered in the Sunday chapter).

Components of a culture of excellence

Seven key understandings seem to be essential to high-performing teams around the world. I would encourage you to explore how you could apply each of these to your own team, refining them as needed over time to suit the make-up of your team and the challenges your team is facing.

As the manager of the team, it is your role to take the lead in creating and sharing the required understandings, and to work with your team to refine them as necessary.

1 Outstanding leadership is key to the team's success

No manager can expect to go into work each day and to act in exactly the same way each time. Your staff must know and accept this – one day you will be firm and strong, another quite relaxed. In addition to becoming a great situational leader, there are many other key leadership styles that you may wish to adopt as needed. Here are three styles that you might choose to learn more about and to use at appropriate moments with your team:

- **Servant leadership:** This style puts the manager in a supporting role, providing support for the needs of the team, without taking an active leadership role.
- **Transformational leadership:** This is an inspirational style, focusing upon helping a team to achieve a vision which is created and formulated by the team's boss.
- **Adaptive leadership:** This style involves encouraging and inspiring a team to recognize, adapt and learn new things to help deal with new challenges facing the team.

You must learn to decide when you should join your team 'on the shopfloor' to help them with their daily operational challenges and when you should step back to take a 'balcony view', seeing the whole picture and thinking strategically about the challenges facing your team.

2 The team always lives up to the highest of values

It is your role as the team's leader to ensure that all of the team aspire to live and work by the highest of values. I cannot tell you what values you should choose, but there are four values that many of today's successful leaders strive to follow with their teams.

- Working with total honesty and integrity
- Working as a single team where individual performance is supported but not at the expense of the overall team
- Only allowing acceptable behaviour and attitudes, with nothing offensive or abusive being tolerated
- Challenging each other to excel and to achieve the most that each person is capable of.

This links to the earlier discussions about culture, and you must allow yourself to lead in creating the optimal environment with the highest of values being maintained.

3 The team maintains a strong culture of learning and development

A successful manager knows that each member of the team is on a personal career path and should wish to help each member to maximize and grow their careers. In addition to gaining experience in their work, a team member needs to grow and develop in many ways. They require your help through:

- assessing what skills and competencies they need to develop
- providing the time and funds for the training they need
- providing them with mentoring and coaching.

Your role as a successful manager will be one of continually helping and encouraging each member of your team never to stop learning, growing and developing.

4 The team changes direction as often as needed

As a manager you must truly accept the need for constant change and help your team to also understand and accept this. Change is inevitable, but failure and poor performance within teams can arise from fighting this need to change and to adapt. Change is not hard if you can create a mindset within your team of acceptance and understanding. Be ready to spend as much time as necessary on communicating with your team about any need to change or adapt that you plan to introduce.

Help your team to understand that they may need to change either *what* they are doing as a team or *how* they are doing things as a team in response to any number of events and actions.

5 **No single team member is greater than the whole team**

I love the following quote from the American baseball player Babe Ruth, which captures the essence of this understanding:

> **'The way a team plays as a whole determines its success. You may have the greatest bunch of individual stars in the world, but if they don't play together, the club won't be worth a dime.'**

A great manager must ensure that the team's drive for excellence is never derailed by an individual in the team – it is better to lose someone from your team if that can serve to maintain the team's overall success.

You will recall the discussion in Friday's chapter about high performers with attitude problems. An excellent manager will not tolerate such staff for long; either the high performer's attitude must quickly improve or they should be asked to leave the team (and organization).

6 The team maintains an optimal work–life balance

A manager must create and maintain a healthy working environment. It is no good if a team achieves its goals through the team members working 18 hours a day and then being off work with stress and heart disorders!

You must also remember to look after your own work–life balance and health. Great managers often work very long hours but take the time to have holidays and to recharge.

7 The team members wish to leave a legacy

What legacy do you and your team members wish to leave behind? Working in a team is not just about earning a salary. We work for about half of the time that we are awake. How can you help make your work together as a team more meaningful and fulfilling? Do discuss such questions with your team.

Encourage your team to help those in the community, bringing your combined skills and experience to benefit those in need. Encourage yourselves to work together in your spare time to do voluntary work of some kind and to have a CSR (corporate social responsibility) impact on your organization and community.

What kind of team do you wish to leave in place? One day you will move on to a new role and/or to a new organization. Will your team members be proud to have worked in your team? What will they recall about the experience in years to come? As you work in your role, try to ensure that you lay the foundation for your team having great memories of being managed and led by you!

What will you do now?

What additional understandings have you thought of implementing? I would encourage you to create an Action Plan for becoming a more successful manager, creating a document such as the following, adding more rows as needed:

What activities and and actions must I focus upon? (Include insights, discoveries, knowledge, theories etc)	Why is a change in this activity or action important for me, my role and/or my team?	How will I practise and ensure this action or activity is improved or implemented? (Include a time frame)

Do seek the support and mentoring advice of your own boss as you strive to become an outstanding leader of your team. Good luck!

Summary

This chapter has shown what you must focus on in order to create a truly sustainable and excellent team.

This book is only the start of your management journey. You must now develop your own style of managing others.

Here are my final three pieces of advice for you as I wish you every success in growing your management career:

Never stop knowing and changing yourself. Be self-aware and observe how you manage others, seeking feedback and being ready to adjust your style as needed.

Always listen to your team. Being a team's manager does not mean that you have all the answers – be ready to humble yourself and to listen to and to learn from your team. They may have more to teach you than you might imagine.

Develop managers within your team. Inspire those in your team to aspire to become great managers themselves in the future. Share what you have learnt from reading this book.

SUNDAY

MONDAY

TUESDAY

WEDNESDAY

THURSDAY

FRIDAY

SATURDAY

Fact-check (answers at the back)

1. What best describes excellent performance?
a) Doing the wrong things well ❏
b) Doing the right things well ❏
c) Doing the wrong things badly ❏
d) Doing the right things badly ❏

2. What is servant leadership?
a) Supporting and letting your team lead ❏
b) Helping your team to achieve a vision ❏
c) Helping your team to adapt to changes ❏
d) None of the above ❏

3. What is adaptive leadership?
a) Supporting and letting your team lead ❏
b) Helping your team to achieve a vision ❏
c) Helping your team to adapt to changes ❏
d) None of the above ❏

4. What is transformational leadership?
a) Supporting and letting your team lead ❏
b) Helping your team to achieve a vision ❏
c) Helping your team to adapt to changes ❏
d) None of the above ❏

5. Why is a culture of learning important?
a) Most people want to grow and develop ❏
b) People will feel valued if their boss supports their learning ❏
c) It will help your staff to perform better ❏
d) All of the above ❏

6. What was my final advice to you?
a) Remain self-aware ❏
b) Listen to your staff ❏
c) Help your staff to grow and become managers one day ❏
d) All of the above ❏

7. What should your Action Plan focus on?
a) Testing what you remember after reading this book ❏
b) Planning what you wish to focus on developing ❏
c) Giving feedback to your staff ❏
d) None of the above ❏

8. Leaving a legacy might involve which of the following?
a) Meeting your budgetary target ❏
b) Hiring new staff ❏
c) Having your team do voluntary work ❏
d) None of the above ❏

9. No one being bigger than the team means what?
a) A team must be large and structured ❏
b) You must hire new staff ❏
c) Mindset and soft skills are important ❏
d) One person cannot be allowed to derail a team's performance ❏

10. What can you learn by really listening to your team?
a) Humility ❏
b) New ideas ❏
c) The team's thoughts ❏
d) All of above ❏

Surviving in tough times

During tough times, you and your team will face new kinds of challenges and uncertainties as your clients and other stakeholders may also be struggling. Your organization may face such difficulties as tight cash flows, declining sales, downsizing and lay-offs of staff. Your managerial skills will be truly tested, but as they say 'what doesn't kill you will make you stronger'. You certainly do not want the tough times killing off your management career as you struggle to lead your team successfully through any difficulties.

Until the recent global economic crisis started in 2008, most of today's managers had never faced a recessionary period during their career and many have struggled to know what to do in the face of the challenges it presents. A common request from their organizations has been to manage their team by 'achieving more with less', meaning that costs and headcount are frozen or reduced while at the same time managers are expected to help their teams achieve more in terms of results and productivity.

This leads to stress and overwork, with employees often only staying in their job because they cannot find another. During such tough times your staff will need extra care and attention as you work to keep them motivated.

1 Help your team overcome the extra stress

When the business conditions become difficult, we can all become more anxious and worried. This can lead to tension, friction and conflict within your team, leaving them in the 'storming' phase. You must rally and inspire your team to help keep them positively aligned and not to allow them to waste any of their valuable time and energy.

2 Work harder than normal to retain your top performers

In difficult economic times your team will have to work harder than usual to achieve its goals and you will need your top performers more than ever. Other organizations may try to headhunt them for exactly the same reasons that you want to keep them: high-performing staff can really help any team through tough times.

3 Do not hold on to poor performers for too long

In tough times you really need the entire team to rise to the challenge and to all perform better. Keeping poorly performing or underperforming members in your team is not ideal. They cost money and their roles would be better filled with someone with more potential to succeed in difficult economic conditions.

4 Communicate openly and honestly

There may be gossip and rumours circulating among your team about topics such as potential downsizing, lay-offs, declining client orders or your company having cash-flow problems. In troubled economic times there may be some truth to these rumours and it is your role as the team leader to be as open as you are able (and allowed to be by your company). Too much negative gossip can be demoralizing and demotivating and will sap the energy of your team at precisely the time that they need to work harder.

5 Keep your team totally aligned and focused on its goals

In tough times, your team might become depressed and lose sight of its goals and growth plans. You must work very hard to motivate, inspire and lift your team to keep the members on track. You may also have to change the targets and goals if the business environment continues to slow down and deteriorate.

6 Look after yourself more than usual

As a team's manager you will face additional stress as you try to help your team steer through troubled times. You may find yourself having to deal with more change and uncertainty and may work longer hours than normal. When possible, step back, take a break and pause to make sure that you are doing the right things with your limited time and energy. Do not overwork and burn yourself out.

7 Spend more time with your team and show empathy

Improve your emotional intelligence and show your team that you care by spending extra time with its members, sitting down and listening to their concerns and troubles. Understand that your team members cannot work well if they are full of concerns and uncertainty. As an empathic manager, you can let them share with you what is troubling them.

8 Work with your team to think out of the box more

Encourage your team to help you solve the new challenges that you may be facing, especially since you may be expected to achieve more with fewer resources (both finances and headcount). You might be surprised by the creative and innovative ideas that your staff come up with if you encourage them to do so.

9 Try harder to motivate your team and to maintain team spirit

Your team members might become quite depressed and despondent in the face of tough times, where all the news and gossip might seem to be negative and depressing. It can get worse for your team if they fear for their jobs. Make time for some motivational and uplifting activities; even if there is less money available, you can still do things with your team.

10 Be more patient and understanding with your team

This may be your team's first experience of a difficult economic environment. They may have no idea how to react to requests to cut costs, to client orders being cancelled etc. You may be in a hurry to implement some changes and new ideas, but you must give your team enough time to understand and to accept the changes that you ask of them.

Answers

Sunday: 1b; 2d; 3c; 4a; 5b; 6b; 7c; 8d; 9d; 10a.

Monday: 1b; 2a; 3d; 4d; 5b; 6d; 7a; 8c; 9d; 10b.

Tuesday: 1d; 2c; 3d; 4b; 5b; 6a; 7d; 8b; 9a; 10b.

Wednesday: 1b; 2d; 3d; 4d; 5b; 6c; 7d; 8d; 9d; 10a.

Thursday: 1b; 2d; 3d; 4d; 5d; 6a; 7b; 8d; 9d; 10d.

Friday: 1b; 2d; 3b; 4d; 5c; 6b; 7a; 8d; 9a; 10d.

Saturday: 1b; 2a; 3c; 4b; 5d; 6d; 7b; 8c; 9d; 10d.

ALSO AVAILABLE IN THE 'IN A WEEK' SERIES

BODY LANGUAGE FOR MANAGEMENT ● BOOKKEEPING AND ACCOUNTING ● CUSTOMER CARE ● DEALING WITH DIFFICULT PEOPLE ● EMOTIONAL INTELLIGENCE ● FINANCE FOR NON-FINANCIAL MANAGERS ● INTRODUCING MANAGEMENT ● MANAGING YOUR BOSS ● MARKET RESEARCH ● NEURO-LINGUISTIC PROGRAMMING ● OUTSTANDING CREATIVITY ● PLANNING YOUR CAREER ● SPEED READING ● SUCCEEDING AT INTERVIEWS ● SUCCESSFUL APPRAISALS ● SUCCESSFUL ASSERTIVENESS ● SUCCESSFUL BUSINESS PLANS ● SUCCESSFUL CHANGE MANAGEMENT ● SUCCESSFUL COACHING ● SUCCESSFUL COPYWRITING ● SUCCESSFUL CVS ● SUCCESSFUL INTERVIEWING

For information about other titles in the series, please visit
www.inaweek.co.uk